Speak or Be Spoken For
A Mic Check Poetry Anthology

Compiled and Edited by Brent C. Green & Ryan McMasters
Art by Katie Call
Prepared for publication by Davis Land

Compiled and edited in Bryan, TX.

miccheckpoetry.org
texasgrandslam.com

contact@miccheckpoetry.org

Poet Check-In:

Preface

From the outside, the famed house called "Poetry" is intimidating.

To most youth in our community, it appears no less than gargantuan, nearly impossible to enter or navigate and almost exclusively occupied by old, dead white men outfitted with pipes and Ph.D.'s. It often seems to the Texas layperson (who might need the craft of poetry more than already-established poets themselves) that the written word is 100 percent occupied and has no space for them.

Mic Check — our humble 501(c)(3) nonprofit in Brazos Valley, Texas — is a front door.

Mic Check is a guest room.

It is a newly-furnished wing in the mansion of creative self-expression.

It is a welcome sign proudly advertising: "You have a voice and your voice is important" in showy, Vegas-style neon.

Mic Check strives to give its Texas community access to the written word on the ground floor. We do so in our free open mics and slam poetry competitions, our festivals such as Texas Grand Slam and Texas Youth Poetry Slam, weekly writing workshops, school lectures, long-term poetry classes at a local juvenile justice center, and more.

Everything we do is another open door and open window. Poetry is a tool of creative, constructive self-expression and should be available to everyone. Mic Check has formed a family around this one foundational idea.

If the house of Poetry has been deemed unfit for living and has been locked and chained by professors and expensive anthologies, that's quite alright. I am happy to report that Mic Check has arrived with bolt cutters and a smile.

We have a voice. Our voice is important. Come on in, you're welcome to stay as long as you'd like.

— Bill Moran
President, Mic Check Poetry (2012-2014)

Amir Safi

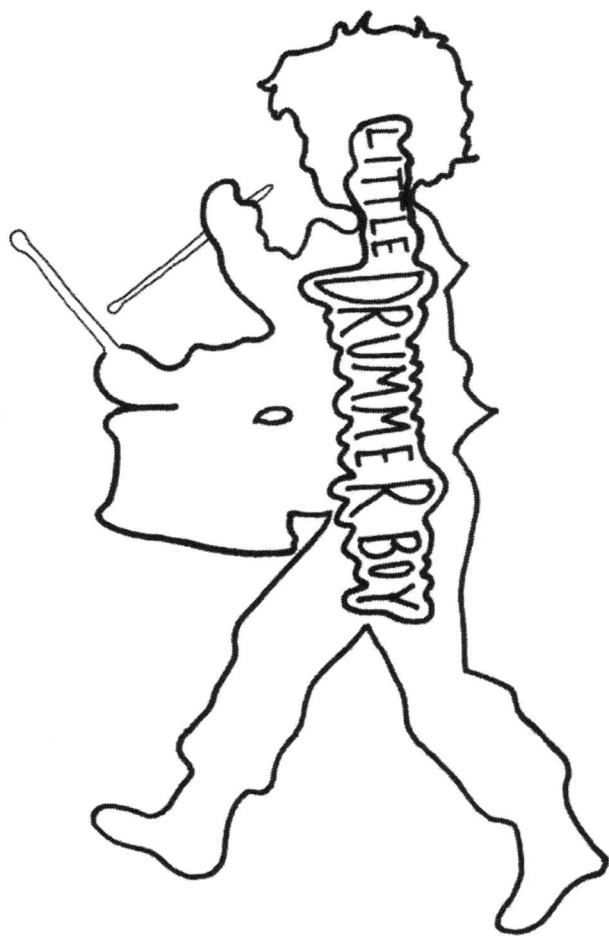

LITTLE DRUMMER BOY

Been to a Few Open Mics

Been to a few open mics,
All of them dim lit.
Seen the happiest of people
Read the most miserable of poetry.
How well they hide under bright eyes
And Friday nights.
I know. I've been there too.

Been to a few open mics,
Some people dim lit from the way a poem can
Ssssssuck the light out of a person.
I know. I've been there too.

When did slam poetry become the news?
A tragic broadcast to yield higher ratings.

I'm sorry. I've been there too.

Audience and Poet,
Reflections of each other.

Feelings precipitate on her cheek week after week
After week.

If this is therapeutic,
Then why do open wounds read the same sad poem
Week after week
After week?

I'm sorry, but we are weak

And I have built a hospice too.

It is therapeutic.
Can't wean off the crutch.
Can a poet get prescribed enough attention?
Pay Attention.

Pseudo Snaps like Pseudo Energy,
We drink it because it's there.
Sugar rushed, now sugar crushed.
Only kissed her because she was there.

[*How do you clap after a poem*
When I still don't know how to feel?

How can you smile after a poem
That just wringed my insides and
Hung them in the backyard?]

I dare you to Blame God One More Time.

Feel better? Did life get better?

Open mics seem to be a great way to hear the whole
Truth of a one-sided story.

I'm sorry. I'm standing here too.

Now, I dare you:

To thank your parents.
Appreciate the kindness of strangers.
Write a poem about the friend you confided in
Who didn't say a word, but just listened and hugged you
Like you were a blanket fresh out of the dryer on a cold day.
Why give this art?

Why give your heart
To someone who is reckless?

Thank the person who wronged you
Because after that experience
You know how to treat people like a human.

Think about a compliment you received and how it made your day. A sincere compliment is okay to re-gift.

Write about the time someone told you they loved you.
You didn't feel the same,
But you were still able to appreciate that they loved you
And you wanted nothing more for their love to be reciprocated
By a better person.

Or about how the girl you're crushing on
Just liked your Facebook status.
And the first thing you thought was,
            "I'm wearing you Doooooooown! Laura Winslow!"

About ice cream cones when your car A/C is struggling,
The perfect joke at the wrong occasion,
Saying hi to the most beautiful girl
While she's got a mouth full of food.
You automatically look cooler.
It's rude.

How sneaking contraband into a movie
Makes you feel like a little bit of an outlaw,
Or about how you and your friends have your own language
And no one else is fluent.

Now write about whatever you want.

There is intrigue in your experience
Whether tragic or triumphant.
But if it is tragic then live triumphantly,
Every breath is a moment toward making it.
After all that you went through you are still here.
You and your magnificent words are someone's
             "It's okay."

There is magic here.
Audience and Poet.
There is joy inside of you.

A raucous laughter.

Get up when it's gray.
When you fray,
There's just more of you.
There is saffron in the sky on a murky day.
Birds will sing you good morning.

Get up and answer the phone next time the bill collector calls.
It's LOVE.
She says you're in debt.

Write her a poem.

"Call it a check with interest."

Been to a few open mics,
All of them dim lit,

And I keep going because
Some things some people say,
I'll carry with me for the rest of my life.

This Heart

This heart is hardly heart-shaped

Hardly, masked crusader long-caped

It is not a construction-paper cut-out.

There is no glitter to hide its ugly.

Unless, you count poetry.

My heart is made of two harps with four strings.

I play my four-stringed banjo harp-heart like a

Drum.

Good Ghost Bill

cities

The Mechanic

An airplane Mechanic in Oklahoma restores 8,000 lb bibles,
presses grease on his tongue
rivets his hands together,
knees to the hangar floor,
and every hour,
prays to God to let his arms become
propellors—
to allow him flight
just once.

The most unbelievable part of this poem is not
that it actually happens—
that God graciously answers his prayers,
or that he flies from
Oklahoma to
Rome
in one shot.

It's the gratitude
he feels up in the air, that I don't buy.
That he does not then wish to become
Wind Itself, and then the
Sun, and then the whole goddamn
Milky Way.
And that his heavy Want
does not
drag

        him into the Atlantic,
        as he begs his God

        for arms
        to swim.

"Polyester" was a famous Greek philosopher.

~~Lafayette Holiday Inn,~~
Olympus, 1984:
Zeus knocks back a fifth of
~~honey whiskey~~ nectar

and blacks out on a pull-out
couch

(his head, too, is polyester,
wet, spring-loaded, queen-sized.)

His daughter, gray-eyed Athena,
famously erupts from his skull

~~hungover~~
battle-weary.

She removes her glimmering,
bronze helmet and

~~vomits on the hotel carpet~~
~~raises four kids in Houston~~

howls with glory.

Madison Wigley

A Wonder of a Woman

Mom got a personal trainer this past year.
He calls her Wonder Woman.

Mom,
It's a wonder
No one has ever called you that before.

It's a wonder
I have never called you that before.

Mom,
I am officially making up for lost time.

You, are Wonder Woman.
And not just for the bullet deflectors you wear around your wrists
But for the bullet holes you wear inside your fists,
From the rounds you've thought were worth keeping,
For the way you still know how to uncurl those clinched fingers
Bullet holes and all.
How you use them to help other people up,
Telling them, "Just think of the holes
As better handholds to grab onto."

Mom,

There was a time when I doubted this.
When I thought you were just some ordinary person.
Like a WWII secretary just following orders
And doing your best to save the world.

But that was before
I had proof
That you bear the Lasso of Truth.
It's not golden like in the comics
But you wrapped it around me a time or two
By just using your eyeballs.

No one ever warned me Wonder Woman could use telekinesis.

Mom,

I know you drove around your little Honda Civic for like ten years.
But I swear you have an invisible jet somewhere.
Because how else would you get to me so fast

Every time I needed you?

Wonder Woman:

I know you lift real weights now.
That your personal trainer has you looking
Like a proper Amazonian princess.

But I know that's all for show
Because your strength never came
From the weights you lifted with your arms
But the weights you lifted with your heart.

Because I know wearing those stars and stripes isn't always easy.
I know how they told you women don't belong on the front lines,
How you stormed the gates anyways.

I know how you sacrificed everything
For the man you thought fell from Heaven
Only to find out he had actually just crashed landed
Because he's a
Really
Sucky
Pilot.

Mom,

I know they never show Wonder Woman crying in the comics
But it's comforting to know that even superheroes have bad days.
Or more honestly
That super heroes rarely have good days,
Because not everyone can be saved.

But I've seen you always try your best, anyways.

You've shown me
Hero-work isn't as easy as dressing up in American flag
And calling yourself freedom.
You still have to deflect a lot of bullets
And sort through a lot of lies
And realize that even though the Steve Trevor's of the world
Can't actually fly
That doesn't mean we can't either.

So, Mom,

Wonder Woman,

I don't know how to help you cope with the people you've lost
Or the pieces of yourself you've lost with them,
I don't know how to heal the bruises around your wrists
With anything but time
And I don't know how to stop the nightmares that happen
While you're not sleeping.

But I do know this:

You are my super hero,
My Amazonian princess role model
And my Friend.
You will always be
A *Wonder* of a *Woman*

Mirrors

Mirrors used to be
For looking yourself all
Up
and
Over

But lately,
My reflection's been staring me
Down
And when I look myself in the eye
All I see is

Demon

So I have grown terrified of Mirrors

The first time I saw them,
Red eyes all flicker,
Like small fire candle sparks
They reflected too much of my *burn* back at me

So I shattered them with my open palms

Only to discover that broken Mirrors
Just make
More
Mirrors

I've never been so terrified.

I've gotta ask
God, are you afraid of Mirrors too?
The last time you saw your demons
Did you shatter them with your hands like
Big. Bangs.

Did you bleed,
As you tried to gather up all the broken pieces
That looked too much like
made in your own image

Are you bleeding still, *God*?

I've gotta ask
Because I've been bleeding for months now

And it took me six weeks
To get around to sweeping up the glass

I did it blindfolded, *God*

The pieces
Were easy to find
Lying around my bathroom sink
I could tell them by their pinpricks

God, I've gotta ask
Are we just *pinpricks*
Lying around your bathroom sink?

Jesus!

I have become
So
Terrified
Of Mirrors!

Like I'm afraid my Demon will look
A little too much like you, *God*

Like I'll discover
David and Goliath is me and my father,
Samson and Delilah me and lost childhood
Moses and Egypt me and that closet

But, *God*
I'm still waiting for that flood

I've built myself an ark fit for sinking

It will sink well, *God*, I promise

Well into the depths of whatever ocean you throw at me

My biggest fear
Is that I
Won't. Drown.
That I will have to face my reflection in the waves

A Mirror
Endlessly
Shattering

Tell me *God*, do you wish that you could drown too?
Is that why you made men in such a way
That they can drown themselves in sorrow?

Do you envy this power that you gave to them?
Is that why you sent your only son here, *God*?

To live out the death you wish you could have had?
Did he disappoint you
When you found out he could
Walk on water?

God, did it terrify you
To see him trailing in your footsteps,
Piercing his palms

On all
Your
Broken
Glass?

God, when we die
Is it you simply digging all the pieces

Out
Of his body?

Or are you still trying to shatter them more?

Scattering our existence into new planes,
New
Mirrors

Are you looking yourself all
Up
And
Are we the demons staring you
Down?

I gotta tell you, *God*

I Don't
Believe
In Heaven

But if such a place exists
I know
It will be Full
of *Drowning*
And Void
of *Mirrors*

Kimberly Weber

Half Price Words

When you find yourself sitting on the floor in the back of Half Price Books debating
purchasing <u>Breakfast of Champions</u> or another bottle of bourbon, you had better
start asking yourself some tough questions:

1) How the hell did you get here?

I mean, yeah,
you remember getting this Diet Coke

you have in your hand,
but it seems to have been perspiring

for a while.

Lapses in time have become

as frequent as lapses in judgment.

2) Do you realize how lonely you are?

These concrete floors

screaming chills into your thighs,
dead mens' words stroking your skull

as you lean into them.

Lean into them,
you need these pages

more than they need you.

These books,

they want something more than your tears
and yet they stay shelved.

3) Why are you still crying?

A blue jazz musician whispers:

> *"Sometimes you have to watch somebody love something*
>
> *before you can love it yourself.*
> *It is as if they are showing you the way."*

Does that apply the same to hate?

4) How does it feel to be useless?

How does it feel to be the part of him

that doesn't help anything?
Help yourself.

5) What the fuck kind of debate is buying alcohol

over pages you've been haunting

this store months for,
at half price,
$7.49?

You would rather contribute another $12 of

insensibility,
senseless and susceptible
to sinking into the sinkhole

you've fostered in your mind,
you stupid girl.

6) Substance abuse is substance abuse.

Regardless of the mood in which it takes place.

If he made you so happy,

why did you so freely fill your belly

with enough blurs, slurs, and stumbles
to forget

that you forgot

how to love yourself?

Your bathroom mirror has caught you

white-pill-handed

more than once.
Sedatives of every sort
hastily shuffled from fingers to lips.
Substance abuse is still substance abuse,

even when you're "happy."

    7) You said you would quit

doing this to your body

a week ago.

Remember that?

    8) You said you would quit

doing this to yourself

two months ago.

Remember that . . . ?

You are pressing depression

into every crevice of your conscious,
asking,

        "Miss Dickinson,

how is that funeral you felt in your brain?"

She responds by shoving "I" and "silence"
and some strange, wrecked, solitary race
down your throat.

Even in death
she swells a tide in your eyes
before rocking back,
and plummeting wordlessly into reason.

Fiona Screams

Fiona screams,
        "They did it all, no thanks to you.
            Because you weren't here."

You are an absentee mother,
you are a Hypocratic Oath of loyalty,
you are a white flag of bleeding wrists —
I mean pens,
I mean,
you are.

Revolution,
you cradled me in your innocent bars
and stars
and starry nights
and damn, he is beautiful,
isn't he?

Revolution,
you feel like a church
all over again.
You are a stage.
You now are staged.
You feel like politics
and dishonest offerings to imaginary gods.
You have been corrupted by favoritism and incompletion.
You are the family I never had the chance to not love.
Here is my revolution.

My heart was spilled for you,
all of you.

My heart,
it aches for you.

My voice screams,
        "But you weren't here."

The first place my voice broke free
was the last place my voice took form.

Love bound by ink-spilled blood
doesn't bind any more than copper floods.
Out of sight, out of mind,
this is where you left me,
drowning on the banks
of the Yellow Sea and home.

I never thought that following my heart
would lead me to persecution.

You taught me that I was free.
But breaking free from late night,
tear-soaked strangleholds felt like
damnation.

How many letters
strung with my own imperfection
must I read
to redeem myself again?

My blood is laced with alcohol.
Thank my father
and swallow once more.

I am better than that.

My heart is laced with apprehension.
Thank my past lovers
and inhale.

I am better than this.

My heart is mangled, tangled.
Thank me.
I tied my own cement bricks

and jumped
and you
didn't even flinch,
oh fair Revolution.

Steve holds Fiona in his arms and whispers,
        "You know,
            90% of the world's problems
            are caused by tiny words
            that come in pairs."

I won't.
He wouldn't.

Regret me all you want,
Revolution.

I was here.

Three years ago
I was here
immortalizing the memories of those long-forgotten,
choking on salvation,
atrophying under the weight of acceptance.

I was here.

                "Fiona takes care of everyone,
                    but no one takes care of Fiona."

No one takes care of Fiona.
Revolution,
no one takes care of you.

Be as true as you were meant to be.

Be *good*.
Be *whole*.

Hafiz says,

                "What we speak becomes the house we live in."

Be more than that,
oh fair Revolution.
Hafiz says,

*"I wish I could show you
when you are lonely or in darkness,
the astonishing light of your being."*

When did I stop being worth that much,
oh fair Revolution?
When did my worth
begin to be measured
by outside perception?

Take care of yourself,
Revolution.
Because no one is here to take care of you.

Bre Breaux

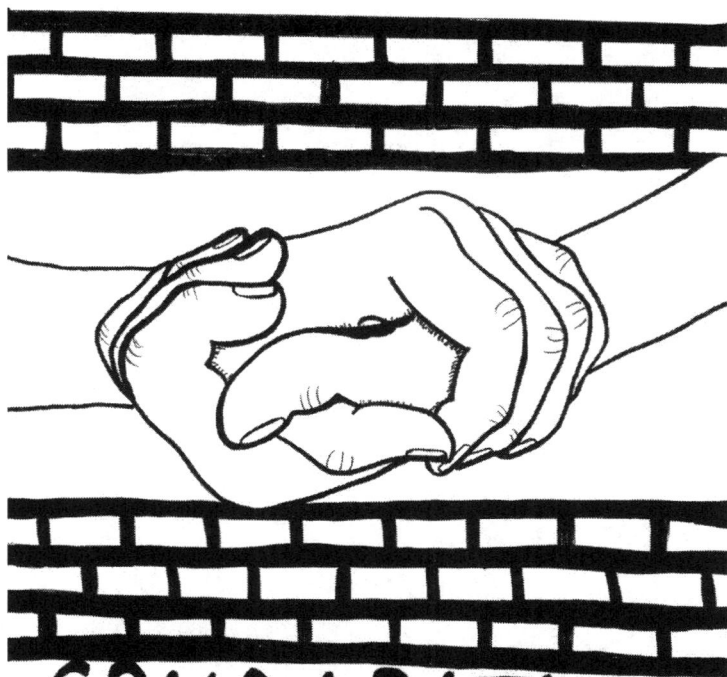

Slouch

Don't slouch your shoulders.

Articulate.
Smile.
Smile **big**.
Smile a lot.
Blink your eyes consciously.
Laugh loud and touch their arm
To show them you're interested.

Don't slouch your shoulders.

Pull them back, stick out your chest,
But not too much.
Put your assets on display, don't give them away.
Don't cross your arms, it sends the wrong message.

I'm pretty sure I told you not to slouch.

Darling, you are a painter.
You have to work hard
If you want anyone to acknowledge your work.

Wide eyes, dear,
Invite them in.
You are a deer,
Capture them in your headlights.
Hide your truck behind those bright eyes of yours.
They'll be blindsided when you hit them
With what you really are
And by then it's too late.
You can take them home to mount them,
Display them to your friends
To prove your accomplishment.

This is your only accomplishment.

This is your life goal:

        Hook a man before your body gives out.
        Use your lying lines
    Before the lines in your skin are too deep for lies.
        You are not human.
        You are a painting.

I am a photograph.
Not a digital picture to be manipulated.
I am not cropped or oversaturated
And I am definitely not filtered.
I am an awkward candid picture
Caught in between phrases,
Eyes half open,
Mouth twisted in a half-grin
I thought I had hidden.
But photographs hold no secrets.
And despite all my teachings
In the art of deception — I mean attraction —

I have managed to continue to slouch my shoulders.

I have always been a broken-backed pianist,
A mad scientist at his organ.
If my piano teacher couldn't get me to sit up straight
I'm pretty sure you won't either.
None of your other advice has ever worked for me.

> *"If you didn't listen to such ugly, harsh music*
> *Maybe boys would like you*
> *Maybe if you wore more girly clothes*
> *Instead of band t-shirts and skinny jeans*
> *Maybe if you looked*
> *More like a girl*
> *Maybe if you didn't cut your hair*
> *Like a boy"*

Well I have let my hair grow.
And it took me a long time
Before I was comfortable wearing a t-shirt in public again.

And yet here I am, single as ever.
Do you have any more *explanations*
Of why guys must find me repulsive?

Maybe it's because I refuse to stop listening
To hard, ugly, beautiful music.
Maybe it's because I hate the color pink.
Maybe it's because I don't bedazzle my clothing to replace
The brightness that no longer lives in your eyes.

What if I told you
I don't want a guy who only likes the way I look?
What if I told you that altering myself is lying,

And it's a terrible way to start a relationship?
What if I told you that I am perfectly happy
Being single?

It took me a long time, but I am.
It used to make me insecure and unsure,
Like there had to be something wrong with me.
But I have ripped that weed you planted in my brain out.
It took a lot of tries.
Every time I would think that thought was gone,
But it would just trick candle past my senses and
Take hold again,
Twist and deprive
My brain of clear thoughts.

But I have finally stomped out your infestation
And when I look at myself in the mirror,
My brain no longer projects
An absence of a body next to mine.
I just see me.

Slouched shoulders and all.

And it is beautiful.

Wings and Guitar Strings

I've got arms full of hummingbirds,
Their hearts beating so fast they're mistaken for tetany.
They are so tense
These filament strings just don't want to let go.

They are tuned to the key of a homesick sorrow
That fuels these itching fingers to trip over strings
So beautifully they call it dancing.

Each step inspires a harmony to my nightmare's culling song.
This guitar vibrates like an M40.
And like my gun,
It makes me feel safe
When my brain is full of bombshells and mortars.
Day after day, dug out in a trench of crowded rooms
Full of worn, sad smiles just as tired of condolences as I am.

40

They call it post-traumatic,
But each day the trauma is as fresh as the battlefield
Blooming in red and white chrysanthemums
In the bodies that have become their soil,
Their roots digging deep,
Branching wounds so they can rest in perforated pieces.

But not me.

I am restless.
The twinkling stars are a million sniper scopes.
The sun sneaks through my window and I see shrapnel.
You can't see my battle scars until I flinch at fireworks.
You see it's hard to trust gunpowder
After seeing it make mosaics out of men.
I am a mosaic of fear and luck and guilt and jealousy.

You didn't have a clean ending, but it was quick.
The doctors stuck a label to my chest
After a quick count of limbs.
It said *survivor*.
It said *fully functional*
When it should have said *fragile,*
Handle with caution,
Explosive,
May contain nuts.

Yes, I still have my arms
But they failed to recognize the buzzing wasp nests inside them.
These stinging memories constantly threaten
To burn more than residual images on my scarred retinas.
So I grab my guitar and let it rock me into peaceful trepidation
And pick out fear one chord at a time.

Brent C. Green

Dove Theory

Officer,
        pointing your gun at me
                        like a foreclosure warning
              on my life
must make you realize
how easy
it'd be
turning
that loaded
gun staring
at my face
into a help-
ing hand.

I dress nice
when I get beaten
by you and this world
to show I mean business
underneath this punk attitude.

When there are no helping hands, only
yelling guns with red lasers
dotted onto my heart
like you think
you can take the heart
out of my convictions.

In untruth's moment
when I'm staring down your gas canisters
that just blinded our protest
I'm still sporting a spotless
birthday suit rental underneath.

One that was ironed
by the judgmental hands of a father
who knew
in sacrificing his humanity
I'd have to make it up for him
and every man with a badge
or superiority complex.

The world is
as it is
because God put a clothes-

line under the Earth,
tilted us over,

                              hung
now we're all hung over— up —on ourselves.

So, policeman,
hang up that badge of a false god you call America.
Stop worshiping a false country,
Uncle Sam doesn't know what's best for us.

He is a terrible Uncle.
I have watched him
asphyxiate us
with his militant hawk culture.

How many doves must be shot
out of the air
after weddings and peace rallies
before the dove takes the eagle's cue
and keeps an arrow tip loaded just in case?

Every backwater ditch on my palm
is a seam holding me together
stronger than the body of congress.

Tied behind my back
I'm held together by clips of skin and
you can't unravel me
by stepping on my back
when I'm down
on the concrete
in handcuffs,
officer.

You need to step
onto the backs
of metaphors instead,
live a little comparatively.

How I know my mind is Tom,
my body Jerry.
Sometimes I have to catch myself
if I want anyone to catch me at all.

So I let the night sky be the history channel rerun
where I know what's next
because I'm a DVR

and fast forwarded to the day I
MAKE history happen.

And that day is today

so I'm fighting you with shattered glass
because I can't stand this world's reflection!

Copyright profits and
false prophets dressed as politicians and
policemen like you
feeding us free-thought options
isn't enough anymore!

I'm standing,
shouting,

"*I am human*!

I am my *own nation*!

I pledge allegiance to *myself*

and *my* well-being.

Who dares

raising a riot shield against this body,
against this movement?

Countries were erected to fight
but fighting back
we're
labeled public traitors

All we want
is to trade this social contract
we did not sign
whose legitimacy we do not accept
for lives of our own.
For lives we want
and lives we dictate
instead of replying "yes, sir"
to our government
acting like
dictators
dictating

                                              our diction

                                    until

                  we don't have the vocab to say,
                  "no, sir" and "fuck you!"

So your gun pointed like that
shows me our human narrative
is a suicide poem
we drive into our brains
with Morse code bullets.

I realize now
how *hard*
it is

to give a helping hand

to the man pointing the loaded gun

at my face.

A Slam Poet's Check on Form

                  Everyone you have seen
                  On this stage tonight
                  Is not who you think.

                  Because it's never people
                  Who grace this ground.

                  Hearts with lips do.

                  Clueless ones
                  Spitting out sculptures
                  Of sound
                  Hoping it looks pretty
                  Inside someone's head.

                  We are the dirt
        Convincing the flawed diamond pieces of ourselves
                  They are still beautiful.

Up here we should never assuage our egos.
We are not be teenage girls
Wanting suicide
So the mortician will make us
For the first time
Beautiful.

We should be here because you listen.

Audience,
These hearts hang their problems
On your ears every week
And never give you a thank you back.

So thank you.

For giving us a platform
Worth standing on.
Without you this stage means nothing.

I've learned
Slam poets can't use props
Because we're supposed to prop ourselves up
With our words.
But we live life off one-liners
And lack the follow-up.

I want the person standing at the mic
After a poem
To be different than
The one who began it.

In the words of Prince,
"We have a job today.
Poets, when you sit to write, remember,
The worst you can do
Is tell the truth.

"If you have the nerve to call yourself a poet
At least believe
The shit you say."

I am calling us out
To better ourselves
From our own words.

We must learn being up here

Does not make us remarkable.
Our stories are not erasable
And we cannot re-mark who we are.

We must see that good writing
Makes us sweat in our chairs
As we write it.
We have to put in work for this!
It's not spilling ourselves onto a page,
That's not writing!
That's the easy way out.
We should not make sloppy work.

The Front Bottoms say
That there is something wrong
In the head of every writer.
That,
"We're artists and our minds
Don't work
The way we want them to."

Is that so often why
Hypocrisy and schizophrenia
Come free with the pen?

I want us to grow
Alongside our writing,
Tell ourselves off
Not just our exes.

To research our heart and
Write a report on it,
Present it to the audience
In less than three minutes,
Let them critique us,
Have ourselves learn from it.

Because if any of us
Were half the person others thought we were,
We'd be twice who we are now.

I feel time grow heavy and thick
When I'm up here.
Do you?
Because there is weight
In this mic
And on this stage.

On this stage
We are not who you think.

We are not sages giving out advice.
We are not stagnant actors.
We are not poets.

We are amateur medicine men
Speaking into sticks
Self-diagnosing our conditions,
Overdosing on our own words.

We are all
Heartbeats
In closed-lid boxes.
Stars
In ill-fitting corpses.
The human condition
Before it is diagnosed.

So die in our writing and rebirth.

As the worst sin we can commit
Is to spit truth
And still be wrong.

Max Kelleher

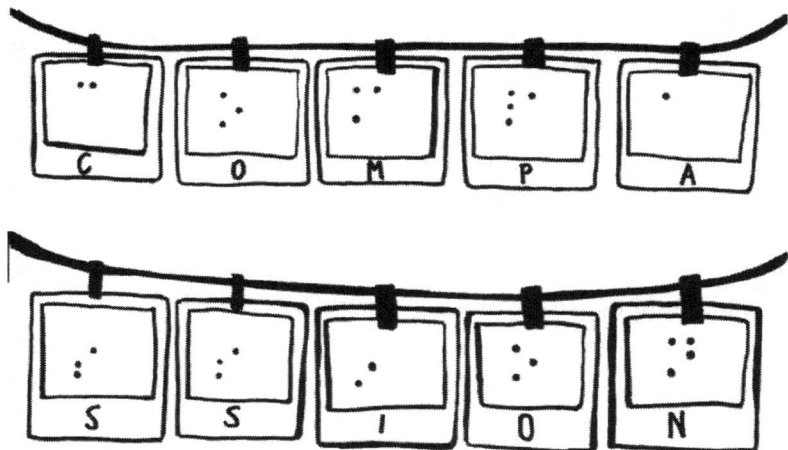

Breathe

Let's trade demons.
I'll give you suicidal thoughts
For uncontrollable rage
'Cause blowing a hole
Through a wall
Can be fixed.
It's more difficult
To replaster a skull.

Red ink on a broken hand,
You'll do better next time.

Breathe

Sara Birnbaum
Was once asked if existing is better than not.
You messed up.
No zombie-apocalypse extra credit.
Sorry,
The suicidal don't get re-tests.

Humans:
We just tend to have sex vertically
Like
We fuck things up.

Breathe

Mirrors don't look like me anymore;
I only recognize myself in
Last-night, fucked-up, filled-cup,
Droopy-eyed portraits
Where a sleepover
Became a hangover,
Completely overt,
Not quite over it.

Breathe

This is not a postcard;
No one wishes you were here.
When it is over,
You will not have a tangible souvenir
To remember this by,

Only the memory of the experience,
If that.
Nothing passes with you
Through the vale.

We are going to die.

Breathe

We have a segmented amount of time
To do something,
Anything,
To benefit future generations
So that they may be able
To benefit humanity as well.
But deep down we know,
You know,
Humanity will end.

The last human will die
On an overcast day,
Fetal-positioned down
On shattered concrete
Surrounded by radiation,
Nuclear fallout.

He will be praying
Inner-head monologue,
Thoughts yelling
Through a mega-phone
In an empty auditorium.

He answers himself,

> *"Give it up, kid.*
> *You were lucky*
> *To get what you got."*

Lungs filling with ash,
He feels it.
He knows it is skin cells;
His friends and family
Gather in his sinuses
For one more hoorah.
It's getting hard to
Breathe . . .

The sky does not part;
Time does not stop;
There is no apocalypse;
Nothing happens . . .
A once loud rock
Now floats silently.
Congratulations,
We mean so much.

Breathe

In the 1960's,
Ford Motor Company
Debuted the Pinto.
But during production
Engineers discovered a major flaw in the car's design.
At 30 miles per hour
A rear end accident would rip away
The tube leading to the gas tank
Sending gas, and I quote, "sloshing
Onto the road around the car."
At 40 miles per hour,
And I quote,
> "Chances are very good that its doors would jam shut
> And its trapped passengers inside
> Would burn to death."
The finical analysis determined
Each human death
To be worth
$200,000.

Breathe

It was concluded
That it was not cost-efficient
To add an $11 per-car cost
In order to correct the flaw.

You can't place
A monetary value on human lives,
But I can't tell
If that's because we are priceless
Or worthless.

Breathe

We are alive

Right now,
Experiencing a reality that
Your 300 million sperm cell siblings
Were not fortunate enough to see.

It is safe to say
That something is happening here
That we don't quite understand.
All of the events of the universe
From the Big Bang
Has led up to us
Showing up here
Right now,
For a moment,
To experience this,
Whatever "this" is.

Yeah
There is something happening here
That we don't quite understand.
So let's take a step back

And breathe.

Blind Traveler

I hope this poem makes you happy.

Thank you
For teaching me
That bridges
Leading nowhere
Should not be burned.
Lately,
It's exactly where I've wanted to go.

You have given me the confidence
To trade in apathy
For a smile,
Follow the genuine of my own voice
To a place where
People speak with respect.
It is everywhere
All the time.

Where people
Do not have to think about death
To find the courage to follow their passion.

Lying motionless
In a blue-lit room,
Xylophone ribcage
Played to my bass-drum-stomach,
Violin bow,
Vibrating vertebrae,
Melody in the way my cheeks
Stretch out like sunsets.
Piano keys on my teeth,
Falsettos on your tongue,
I hear you.

It sounds like we made it.
We have won.
All of it.
The whole damn thing.

Blind Traveler,
You are a citizen of the world.
You have Norway in your scars,
Virginia in your smile,
Africa on your left cheek,
Qatar in your voice,
Portugal in your fists,

Dallas on your lips.

Sometimes we need an example
Before we believe in the extraordinary.

You will laugh at your fears
When you finally find out
Who you are
And what you do;
You are so close.

And I mean that.
You are close to me
Like oxygen;
I feel you in my throat.
Fill airways with hope
So that when I exhale on the base of your neck
It will give you something to believe in,

Like light exploding off everything it touches
Just so we can see
Reflection,
You blind traveler.

You are close to me.
It's too bad some never get the chance
To know the answer to the question
Neither of us wants to ask.
Timid philosophers
Thirsty for knowledge,
We are too afraid to pursue.

Like putting both our life savings on red,
Spinning the roulette wheel
And walking away
From it all
Fingers interlocked
Because it doesn't matter;
We never needed dead presidents.
We make our own happiness.
Always have.

Blind Traveler:

Don't say it
If you are not ready.
Especially
If you don't mean it.
I might not be your destination;
I might be a full tank of gas
Helping out a blind traveler.
Make me more than an interesting stop on your journey.

Sentient Traveler,

I hope you print this out,
Fold it into a memory,
Staple it to the inside of your eyelids
And think of me when you close them to rest.
See me in your dreams.

I hope you read this
In five years
Just before your first day
At a dream-job-hospital.

I hope you remember this
In fifteen years
As you fiddle with your wedding ring
And have to bite your bottom lip
So people don't ask why you are smiling.

I hope you unfold this
In thirty years,
The day your second child
Leaves for college
And I hope you smile when you read it.
I hope you are smiling;
Honest,
I do.

I hope you read this
And remember.

Remember
Not who I was
But who you are.

Inspiration,

You were an earth-child gunslinger.
You had loaded muse
And compassion
Into your revolver,
Shot at me when I wasn't looking.
It took me a while
To dig them out of my gut
But I got them.

Blind Traveler,

Take my hand,

Hop on my bike;

We're going home.

Rae Harris

nature.

I WANT TO OVER-WHELM YOU. BE SO MUCH MYSELF YOU HAVE NO CHOICE BUT TO STARE.

nature.

Nature.

nature.

If and Instead

If I were a man, I'd be tall and thin

With eyes as clear as ice

I'd only be strong enough to carry myself

I would be an artist, I'd never sell out

I would be comfortable with my past

I'd be the corner of my living room

Where I fit perfectly,

Where honesty drapes my windows

As a man, I would no longer be the chair that holds up each person who just needs a rest

They would become the ottoman beneath my feet

Instead, this is myself:

Strong enough to hold others in the full attention of my arms, only leaving one spare finger for myself

Deep eyes, soiled with my past

I am only an artist when it is comfortable

I cannot dream long enough to let my art drive me

I am always awakened by my sense

In reality, I am a business woman. I will sell out.

I will be profitable. A future wife and mother.

I realize I will serve with my life. Serve my family, my children, my man, my God, my father.

Serving, but not satisfying

My past and I refuse to speak to one another

As a man, I could afford an oasis

As the woman I am, I must stay a stable desert

With no room for weeping storms knocking on my window,

Its racing heart pleading to beat down my door

I will hold you all day as you spill out your love and your pain.

I will give you my advice and my ears

But do not ask for my return. For I only give my mouth to the men I wish I was

These men become my idols.

I plan to become them and spoil them until I can become what I should be.

Regardless of what they deserve, they'll get all of me

I at least deserve to be around them to create the happiness I should possess by supporting and conjuring their contentment and approval.

As I live vicariously through them, I will treat them like the king I wish I could be.

Wearing my heart as a crown, high above where others could reach

Home

Bright smile behind cracked lip

God forbid we show our weakness

Better to threaten me and flex your weapons

We appreciate men for their bravery
Love women for their reactions

But that is all pretense, a way to feel less alone

You want to be wanted
I need to be needed

People call me beautiful like a name
I speak with sass and jazz-hand-shrapnel

My lips should be lined with light pink smiles; not bright red opinions

I am too tall, too man-hands,
Willing to see the world from above average height with changed view,
strutting in heels at six foot two
My hands being bigger than yours doesn't scare me
They show ability to hold as much as yours

These eyes speak more than you'd ever want your woman to
Intelligence and ambition are only endearing when they don't challenge a
husband,
I am too loud-mouth and quiet clothes,
A short skirt without a promise
Too open and sexualized
For a woman

You tell us dress modestly, show power quietly
Confidence doesn't have a mute function

You may need to strap on your helmet, shrapnel is bound to follow

Teach yourself a lesson in love, starting with your body
Eyes should be the window into soul
Mouth a door to mind
Your only defense is to dress them

Decorate them with cloth and color

Become a painting
Don't be afraid to be too honest
Paint yourself
Become your own masterpiece

The most beautiful poem you've ever written is your skin

I want to overwhelm you
Be so much myself, you have no choice but to stare
Too much into real, too much out of romance and fairy tales
Too much independent, not enough I need you
These bright lips were made to love, not to yell
These man-hands to hold, not to fight
They can see fire through windows
I am a house without windows
You can't become a home until you love your walls
I am a home without windows
Sealed doors and well-woven tapestries
Only opened with purpose

Don't be a shelter for others,
Build a home for yourself.

Greyson Holt

alienation.

Lion Heart

Behold: Greyson, the Lion-hearted!!!

A courageous man! Good-looking and highly regarded! With a dashing smile and charm for miles!

His capabilities simply can't be charted.
He's the guy you want to bring home to your father, the one you don't want to let get away.
He's the one that scares the opposition, a wild card when it's most needed.
He's the surge of epinephrine you got when you and your lover first greeted.
His words, they dissolve like honey, reviving any soul who feels defeated.
He can do more than your mind dares to conceive.
He's willing to face any brand of distasteful death if he can only hold fast to what he believes.
He doesn't mind a departure from Earth as odd as at the hands of Sweeney Todd.
And he'd revel in passing away like one of the prophets, even Stephen
Who was stoned to death as a martyr.

Unfortunately, I'd rather be . . .

stoned to death than to cauterize the gash from which flows my bleeding soul. A doughnut of a man with a sweet exterior, yet these glazed eyes can't hide the fact that I'm not whole.

And now, behold: Greyson with a lying heart.
A man who from the stated ideology would quickly depart
Any meaningful lifestyle I'd rather talk about than start.
I'm the guy who can't get past hate for his father,
The one who let his true love get away.
I am terrified of opposition,
A plastic wild card for a back that melts when things get heated.
I'm the destitute look in your eyes
When you discover your lover cheated.
I'm the sweet dream that starts but never gets completed.
I'm absolutely terrified of what I *won't* achieve.
I'll die a thousand times if only I can continue to deceive.
And when I depart from Earth it's quite odd,
Because even though I get higher
It seems like I can never find
my . . . my . . . where is my damn . . .

Light.

Realization set in I've been spending my life hating myself for not fitting in.

I'm a teenage girl vomiting her insides 'cause she feels she doesn't fit her skin.

I'm innocent eyes watching pornography and having sex too young to fit the stereotype of "men."

I'm the alcoholic whose world is out of control so he drinks to match his head with its spin.

I'm the wealthy aristocrat whose income is fat but satisfaction is thin.

I'm the gamer whose entire self-worth is wrapped up in being top assassin.

I'm the abused wife who tries to fill the role of heroine.

I'm your ex-lover . . . who you're addicted to . . . like heroin.

I'm the man who has whittled his soul down to the smallest stroke of a pen.

And now I'm the man who will no longer let the borders of this page act as a pen.
I'll stand up and tell my story to receive redemption for my sins.
As you read this poem we share a heart; that makes us kin.
So I put a round in the chamber, and put to death my evil twin.
And now I'll go on smiling, grinning this goofy grin.

'Cause *this* is who I am.

Everyday Low Standards

I was walking out of Wal-Mart when I was stopped dead in my tracks by the most beautiful thing I had ever seen.

The sky was a symphony of color. Purple melted red, glowed orange, danced pink. I slowly sunk into the sunset only to be pulled out again by the horrible realization that NO ONE ELSE AROUND ME NOTICED.

Fury flamed up inside of me and I screamed: "When did we drop our gaze from the beauty of the sky?! How did our dreams plummet to less than six feet high?! Mirrors of the six feet under look in our eyes?!"

A startled man looked in the direction I was pointing. I could tell he was near-sighted when he responded: "I hate those things. Filthy," referring to a grackle that had flown by.

I handed him the notecards I had bought and said: "I understand that you're unhappy and you're not sure why. I'm telling you, brother, we too were born to fly."

Dave Jones

My valiant Persian foes:

Know that I, Peter, stand between you and victory!

* * * * *

I, Peter, shall not let them pass!
I shall be like three hundred men or more.
Their arrows and slings I shall not fear,
for they will fall, harmless, at my side.

They number thousands,
but I, though one, am millions.
For the spirit of Pan generations lives in my soul.
I will uphold the honor of my great green-tighted ancestors.

Like Wilbur Pan,
who put one of his eyes out
before dispatching the greatest of the cyclops warriors
(so it would be a fair fight!)
I will both honor my enemies
and defeat them!

As Admiral Susanna Pan sailed the world
seeking the mightiest to crush with her hammer,
I will bravely rush my doomed opponents.

I, Peter . . . Peter Pan . . . I . . . i . . . I . . .
TODAY . . . *I am INVICIBLE.*

. . .

CRAP! I hope Tinker Bell gets here soon.
I'm about to shit my tights!

WHAT would it MEAN?

WHAT would it MEAN?

The sounds we speak and the scrawlings we write may be formed to symbolize meanings.

But one can speak more loudly, deeper, clearly, in a language that spans space and time.

As if it were poetry from before the dawn of time

written into the fabric of the universe,

it speaks in ways our utterances and writings never could.

WHAT would it mean?

What could we and would we

say if we spoke this language tonight?

Would it be beautiful?

Would it be music that burns in our hearts forever?

Or would we cover our ears and yell, "I can't hear you!"

trying to drive it away?

But we cannot drive it away — it speaks directly into the core of our beings.

What would it mean?

What could we and would we

say if we spoke this language tonight?

Would it have a creative force?

As God spoke the world into being will we proclaim,

"Let there be something here more than was here when we started,"

with such force that what we speak becomes reality?

Or will we proclaim division and opposition?

Two opponents playing a game,

having fun, perhaps, but proclaiming,

"Let me defeat the other, taking what I can,"

with such force that the world is less than what it was when we started?

WHAT would it mean?

What could we and would we

say if we spoke this language tonight?

You and I together making music that shakes the stars in the heavens

and rumbles the pillars that hold up the earth.

Would it be something worth saying?

Would the stars burn brighter?

Would the Earth resonate and dance joyously for the rest of our lives?

Or would a surge of intense, passionate

. . . banality

suck the life out of a star?

And isn't that what we often do?

USING this language

and USING each other

voraciously consuming, unsustainably

in something we call love.

But is it?

WHAT would it mean?

What could we and would we

say if we spoke this language tonight?

I don't want us to open our mouths and

shout out to all creation

   absolutely

     nothing

at all

worth

saying.

So what would it mean?

It would mean nothing to speak of.

You're beautiful and sexy and a lot of fun.

But you and I have nothing to say worth saying.

So why don't I just give you a ride home and a goodnight hug?

I'll call you sometime.

I hope you're not disappointed.

Let's keep gazing at the stars;

maybe,

someday

you and I will have something to say

that will make one of them burn brighter.

Sarah Maddux

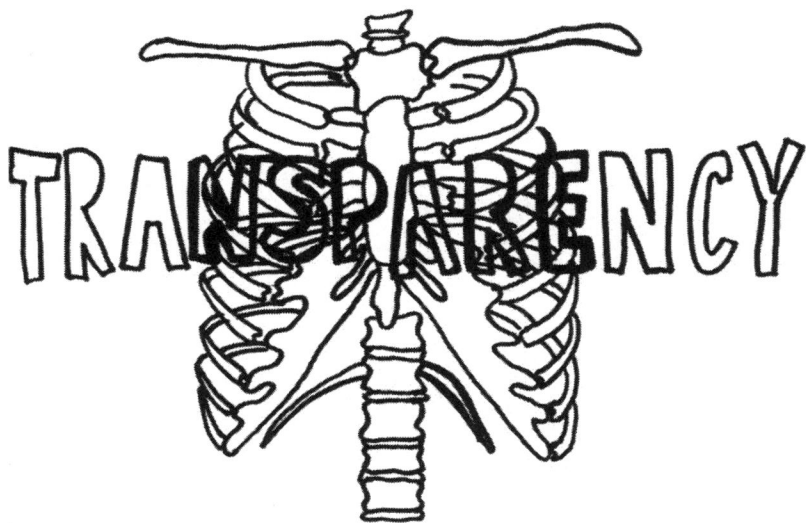

TRANSPARENCY

Peter

I don't know what prompted my classmate to shout,

"What kind of name is Peter anyway?"

And I don't know what lapse of reason
Or social etiquette
Prompted me to reply,

"The name of my stillborn brother."

I did,
However,
Understand the horror on her face
As she realized that she had just made
The worst social blunder of her young life.
And as strange as it may sound,
I can explain why I started to laugh

Uncontrollably,

While everyone watched in dismay
At the train crash
Exiting my mouth.

You see,
Knowing that you exist
Only because someone else doesn't

Is awkward.

When you're born to fill a space in hearts carved out
For another child,
The love never quite fits right.
It's uncomfortable,
Hand-me-down shoes that have never been worn,
Sleeping in someone else's bed.

When people comment on the unusually long age gap
Between my older brother and me
The ill-fitting awkwardness shakes loose
And comes pouring out of my mouth disguised
As a fountain of nervous

Laughter.

Maybe it would be different if he'd been my younger brother.

If my handprints were already immortalized
In plaster on the mantle
When my grandfather
Built a tiny pinewood box in the backyard.

Maybe I would be able to mourn
For him then
Without feeling like I'm betraying myself.

Maybe I wouldn't feel like I'm betraying my family when I don't.

I don't know how to miss someone
I would never have gotten the chance to meet.

But sometimes,
I wonder how different things would have been
If nature hadn't dealt him a hand
From a deck

So many cards short.

Would he have been the linebacker my uncle always swore
My parents would have?

Would my sister have wished for a princess
To dress for church on Sunday mornings?
Or would she have been tougher
With four younger brothers to corral?

Would my older brother have bonded better to him
Than to a set of blonde curls
That stole his limelight just when he was old enough to miss it?

Would his name even have been Peter?

Would my father have been able to look at him
And see his own restless eyes staring back at him

The way mine do?

Would he finally have been able to give up his own name?

Would my mother cry less?

Would he have been better at keeping his fingers
Away from electric fences
Charged with tradition and family loyalty?

Would he have given her the grandchildren
She's afraid I never will?

Would the old oak tree under which he is buried grow as tall
Without his soul cradled in its roots?

Would my family have run more smoothly
If none of the parts were replacements?

Would my parents ever wonder if their family was out of balance?
What it would have been like to have another daughter?

Would they have had another daughter?

Would they miss me?

I would like to think so,

But I laughed.

And I think that means no.

Starting Route to Hypocrisy

1. Find something to believe in.
    For convenience sake
    Take the road most familiar;
    It makes for a smoother ride.

2. Do not put your faith in it.
    Put faith only in yourself.
    Make believe it is all under your control,
    That choosing a road means you know how to drive.

3. Establish a monopoly on truth.
    You do not have to be right.
    You just have to shout the loudest.

4. Make up your own rules.
   Apply them to others only.
   Everyone knows
   Highway patrolmen
   Do not have to drive the speed limit.

5. When you fuck up,
   And you will,
   Tell no one.
   Turn heartbreaking into hit and run,
   Rollover into run away.
   If people are going to find out,
   Tell everyone.
   Turn wasted opportunities into well-earned wisdom,
   Tragedy into testimony.

6. Realize that you have no idea where you are going
   Or why you are going there.
   Engage autopilot.

7. Learn to sing with your throat sewn shut
   To hold in the screams,
   To smile over blood-stained teeth.
   Mask the smell of scorched rubber
   With offerings of incense and indignation.

8. When you run out of gas
   Drive off a cliff.
   Take anyone along for the ride down with you.
   The more hearts that burn
   The brighter the explosion.

9. Do not apologize.
   Or do.
   It does not matter.
   Words cannot wash blood-stained glass windows

10. Limp out of the wreckage.
    Climb back up the cliff.
    Hitch a ride on someone else's dreams.

    Repeat steps 1 - 10.

    Or don't.

Instead

Throw away the road map.
Rip the GPS from the dashboard with bloodied fingernails.

Walk away.
Find out what your feet are for.

Learn to bushwhack,
To read the stars in your own eyes for directions.

Keep moving or stand still long enough to breathe.

Remember that

You don't have to be going somewhere

To find yourself.

Alex Gaston

I'm Sorry

He said he'd love me always.
I could not say the same.
His lips spilled secrets over the mountain of our pillows,
Whispers only in the refuge of the dark.
I could not offer my own
For fear of their ugliness even in the shadows.
He laced sincerity in every touch,
In every kiss placed delicately on my cheek.
I'd wipe them off with the back of my hand
Unsure of the reason I didn't want them to stay.
He threaded his fingers into mine;
I tried to unravel them gently.
To be woven into his palms,
Stitched into the fabric of his skin
Proved to be a nearness I could not bear the weight of.
All he wanted was to love me.
I could not bring myself to want him in return.
He offered me his heart.
I could not do the same.

I Do Not Understand

I am not color blind.
I see the differences that separate us.
I understand that we come from two separate worlds.
I was raised with the delightful concept that everyone is equal.
You were raised by the searing whip of truth.
I was born into a life of privilege and consequential naivety
While you learned how to survive
In the reality of our broken culture.

Some things I will never be able to understand.
Empathize with, perhaps, but never truly comprehend.
While we lie in bed at night, our skin melding together
Underneath blankets that capture our wanting breaths,
Our worlds collide.
And your stories shock me.
How can we walk down the same street,
But experience two starkly different realms?
You spill realities of our double-edged culture,
Things that, in my world, happen only in the wickedest of places.

Things that, in your world, happen on a frequent occasion.
These injustices spill from your lips to my ears
And mark out the miles that distance us.
And I realize that "my people" are the problem,
And "your people" are the problem.

I am not color blind.
I see the differences that separate us.
But these broken pasts do not have to define our futures.
I do not understand how our worlds remain divided,
How the people of my skin cannot see the beauty in your skin,
The beauty that radiates in the dark depths of your lovely exterior,
And the beauty that exudes from underneath.
Can they not see that, no matter the fabric of our skin,
We are all woven from the threads of the same human condition?
I do not understand the contented ignorance
And passivity of our people;
I do not understand our worlds.

Elizabeth Ashley White

Galaxy Slums

A tourist,
>> he ends up in the wrong hotel room,
>> sits down for a while.
He says, "You should take walk down the beach
>> at midnight,
>>> alone."
Kicks off his shoes.
He's an astronaut.
He knows things,
>> like real smart things about real big things
>>> with long names.

I know about happiness andthe stars sometimes.

>>> The sun looks funny when you squint and
>>> Kinda like looking down the barrel of a
>>> gun when it
>>> fires.
>>> Lights up your world,
>>> baby girl
>>> this tourist brought his camera
>>> this astronaut brought his space suit.
>>> Doesn't want to get too close but he'll
>>> remember every
>>> bit of you
>>> by all the pictures he took.

cock you head to one side

Galaxy slums.
Like where the stars aren't as bright.

>>>> I just want to be happy
>>>> like I've seen all the stars.

I look him in the eyes and ask him
>> where he's been and he just
> s i g h s   r e a l   h e a v y.

Kicks off those astronaut shoes.
Still in the wrong hotel room and
I'm walking along the beach the water's still.
Real quiet,
I can see the stars in it,
underneath it.
The water and the stars and
>>> you.
Staring at it.   Pulling at it with your hands,

making the bed is significantly easier with someone
helping you.

I helped you with your astronaut shoes
because you constantly fought with
g r a v i t y.
Picking arguments with it as if it talked back.

It does.

Says "Up," and "Down" and "No,
listen to me,
down here on earth I make the rules,
you're not an astronaut here."

Almost a year ago, I met a spaceship.
Hadn't been outside the atmosphere for
a while, gray because he was a little dusty,
carried some baggage, nothing he hadn't
already unpacked yet. Said, I've been
waiting here for a while
baby girl.

He put his hands on my hips,
and didn't let me go when I needed him to most.

It took me 21 years to realize that I don't want spaceships,
I don't want   astronauts.
I want someone that is used
to gravity, someone that
can feel the pull of
my heart
on
theirs.

I fell in love with my best friend.

We stargaze together.
We laugh in planets
and speak in galaxies.
He's my
every-shooting-star-wish
come true.

I'm so happy like,
never seen so many stars.

Morgan Frazier

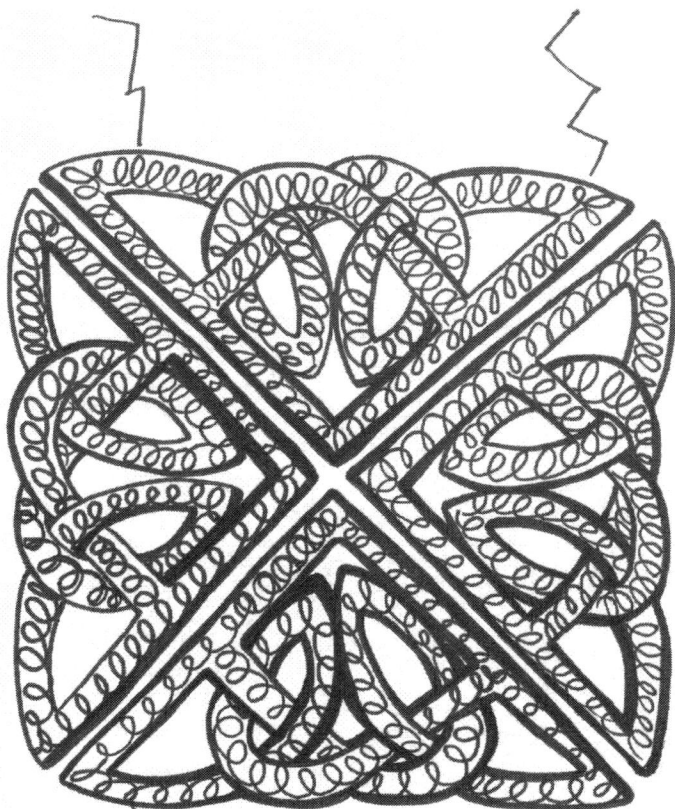

Fionn's Knot:
A celtic representation of
COURAGE

Why Bluebonnets Go Dormant

The death of true love
          Is not a pretty girl
                    Lying in a glass coffin
                             In the woods.

It is an ugly drunk
Passed out in the
Charcoal-ashes
Of bonfire dancers.

It howls
75 miles per hour down I-40.

It kisses
Like gravel under tires.

Pennsylvania!
Is an angel
Falling black gold, tar, and
Heaven-feathered,
Whistling through the wind
Like mockingbirds.

Texas!
Is a back-road sunset
Dancing down our spines.

Death . . .
Is a boy and a girl
With their lips still dyed bluebonnet,
Cheeks still stained with sunrise,
Eyelashes dewdrop-heavy.

We were never meant to be perfect.

Just beautiful.

Love
Is a bluebonnet
Growing through the cracks of I-40.
Even though it fights with its own foundations,
Loving even when these tires
Mulch and
Roll and

Bleed out every drop of sunlight left in you.

Love
Is letting love happen anyway
And calling this
Disaster
Fertilizer.

This is an investment.
This is a mosaic
Of bed sheets
To keep you warm
Up north
In that head of yours.

Our blood paints
A bit like a Texan midnight
Down your medians.
It slicks a bit
Like oil on wedding bands
And phantom tongues.

Did you know?
That the highway out of town
In the summer
Smells a lot like,
        "I still love you."
Every winter it cracks more,
        "I'm sorry."

But we all know by now
The season in Texas changes
Daily.

So I'm sorry if
I still act confused,
And forget to ask myself why sometimes.

I'm sorry
My roots couldn't hold you
Together better.
I'm sorry
I keep saying sorry,
But I don't know
Any other
Way to
        "I love you"

Anymore.

I don't know
How to smile at you
Without apologizing anymore.

I can't stop
Feeling guilty for not
Letting go
As easily as you
Anymore.

       "I love you! —
I mean,
       I'm sorry."

I'm not . . .
Very good at caging
This lion of a fist fight in my chest
Anymore.

She growls,
Hungry,
Says your logic tastes
A LOT like bullshit,
Tries to punch a hole
Through my ribcage.

Says,
       "How can you complain
       About another raging empty
       When this was never whole
       To begin with?

       Stop trying to replace something
       That was never missing.

       You wanted wild.
       Why don't you skydive
       Off these broken pieces
       Of "I TRIED!" already.

       75 miles per hour!
       Let it howl!
       Let it hurt!"

. . Because
Bluebonnets will still grow
Wherever they land.

It's not your fault
The highway was one of them.

Texas! . . .
You always had
Too big of a heart
To hold your own weight.

Laura Lynn Phillips

DIRECTION

Blaming You Goodbye

Memories of you made me hide your books away,
Scared you would take them
Like the time you took my heart
And made me take it back.

I keep finding you.

                                    In every day.

In every "i love you."
With every lowercase "i" dotted with too much heart.

Yesterday I said "goodbye."
I've never had to say that to you before.
The word tasted like regret falling into a casket.

Listening to your mother weep, I blamed you.
Praying in Korean, I blamed you.

I blamed you, for so long.

I should have realized.
The warning signs were all there
Reflected like an "I yield" sign.
I should have known you were the casket I built.
I hide it between my shoulders

And I couldn't help but blame myself.

So today I hid your books
To keep you from ruining
Another story book ending.

You were my Romeo,
But you waited for your Juliet too long,
Drinking your poison before she could stop you.

Now she's living in her tomb
While you're buried in the casket you built,

Wearing a headstone like a crown
Labeled with too much heart.

Davis Land

bus poem

there is a dead bird on the road
next to the bus stop
i am stepping on to the bus
the bird is covered in bees now
the person i am sitting next to does not know i am typing a poem
the bird does not know it is now covered in bees
my phone rings but i am not going to answer it
because it would bother the other people on the bus

Apple Trees

i'm having a big party tonight with lots o

chandelier and even more

champagne

got shot glasses and ash trays lined up like apple seeds

just a short clip of I-35 and a few

matchsticks

away

got it all layed out in print,
right in front of me,
sayin',

"

Extra! Extra!
Tonight! Sunset! Biggest Event of the Year!
Man Duels Himself for A Girl!

and   *he*   *loses!*

chops himself up into bits in front of everyone and goes down
without a fight!

it's magnificent!

you gotta be there!

"

.
.
.

and this is why we have those apple seeds

to bring my friend back down to earth again

bring him up

forests light themselves on fire to be born again and
tonight
bud,

we got a lot of burnin' to do
a lot of forests in our throats and our chests

all the highways and the dumb chandeliers

(we're gonna swing on em')

till our lungs fall out and you have her

painted

all over the place

gonna throw our arms through panes of glass like

nothing can hurt you more than she did

'cause nothin' can

we're gonna use these
hearts for
what they were meant for

we're gonna yell down I-35 at ninety miles an hour

and *hope*
for some answer back

because

here,
friend,
with us

you don't bury your feelings

you drown them in gasoline and light them on *fire*.

Christian Taylor

ANDROGYNOUS

Go out

pluck mornings from tomorrows

                              go out

leave now

        coffeeless and throbbing

dance yourself bloodless on shards of new conversation

        talk alleys into sleeping with you

please, tonight have all

hear:

the corner bar bohemia of a sixties hick

the mouths burning Owsley acid into morning breath

the southern crawl from your voice box

please don't touch the gangs out here

waddling off stories in slurred words

shut up

learn the language of shoe

chat up some single-mother-street and her lace and her panties

study her untied humanity

until the restaurant orchestra retunes once more

until Saturday Texas leaves for work in the morning

Kristy McNulty

TRUTH

Puppeteers and Souvenirs

You know you can't live without heavy metal?
In This Moment
Trace elements of iron, copper, and zinc
Are clog dancing through your arteries
And without them, you would cease to exist.
But for metalheads like myself,
This phrase has a whole new meaning.

Heavy metal is peculiar like that.
It's an essential nutrient found in our bodies,
But also a misconstrued genre of music.
Both make your heart race in large quantities
And are fatal if you let them consume you
Rather than the other way around.

Metallica's Master of Puppets
Is one of their fastest albums ever produced,
The title track's drums averaging 186 beats a minute,
The same rate the human heart beats when excited.
Sometimes it's from getting Bourbon-Street-on-Mardi-Gras-drunk,
Or Andromeda-Galaxy-high,
Or adrenaline electrifying your blood every time he touches you,
Which can sometimes all feel the same.

I remember the first time I saw him,
It was mid-October
And I was midway drunk
Before I could work up the nerve to talk to him.
He looked at me with Neptune eyes
That exploded into supernovas with colliding stars;
I forgot how to breathe.
And I felt this amplifier heart spark with static
From all the skipped beats.

See, what people don't realize is that hearts and heavy metal
Aren't so different in how they operate.
When it's lifeless, you have to jolt the electricity back into it,
Jumpstart that Kona in your chest
Until it pop-punk punches back to life.
And never let it flatline again like I did.

I let this standstill Kona stay unplugged for too long.
I was a poet losing grip of her pen,
Feeling inspiration escape my fingers

As fast as the man that left me before you,
Flipping sheet after sheet of blank pages for eight months.
I was a solo power chord waiting for its other half,
For a tonic that didn't sound so dissonant.
I was diminishing as fast as a seventh chord falling flat
Before your fingers strummed C major back into these Gibson veins.

With you next to me,
I could feel our hearts beat in thrash metal symphonies,
Too fast and too loud for most people's first listening,
But never complete without the silence in-between.
And when you laid your head beside me
I wondered if you felt the Rickenbacker bass
Plucking at my four heart strings
Or the Mapex drums in my chest
Beating as fast as I felt myself falling.

My only regret now is not speaking up.
I should've learned
How to use the adjustment knobs on this amplifier,
Turned down the distortion and turned up the reverb,
Let you hear me loud and clear
With no more bullshit to drown me out.
This Cabernet bottle just couldn't uncork
All the words I wanted to say.

But I was able to part these glass lips
From that airtight vacuum
Every time you kissed me.

I wanted to tell you more.
Like,
    "I miss you.
    I miss you like constellations that miss the sun
    When dusk has faded."

Now, I only hope you knew what I meant
By the way I sparkled from the oasis
You put back into these arid desert eyes;
You finally made them green again.
Or by the way I laced my body with yours
Until we were no longer two distinct instruments,
Just a single double-necked Fender.

Thinking back to the nights we had
I wish I had gotten to know you more,
That I could've learned your heart

As well as I learned the curve in your lips.
I didn't just want to hear your poems
But also the stories behind them.
I want to go back to that night and remember how it felt
To look at you for the first time again,
How it felt like . . .
My heart plugging itself back in.

But here I am again, without you now.
And on these Sunday nights I drive down highway 6,
Back to where we first met,
And I wonder where you are tonight.
I feel the wind take my breath away.
I look to the sky and swear I can see Neptune
Waiting to collide with nearby stars.
And it's almost like you're here again.

Can't Spell Prejudice without Red

She tells me red is her favorite color.

It's bold,
Energetic,
Dangerous.
The color of roses,
Hearts,
Hell.

Its warning signs
Telling others to stay out,
Used to cross out particular things
To tell you what is and is not acceptable.

Every day she prances
In her favorite red dress and red stilettos

As she Triceratops-stomps
Across the Lone Star state
Ready to *cross* out more people
As she totes her own gaudy *one*
Around her neck.

She says,
        "I see now why red is the color of choice
        For Republicans.

I want to be the face of them all
Even if it means I have to
Ride an elephant with Rick Santorum
At the Republican Convention
In the most redneck,
Gun-totin',
Backwoods state in the South
Trampling anyone that gets in my way.

After all, red is my favorite color.
Especially when I see a Democrat
Covered in it."

She tells me this while showcasing
The churches on her skin
That conceal every inch of her body,
So proud and oblivious
To how many people she could have
Taken off the streets
With money spent building
Her extravagant chapels.

Arrogance and ignorance
Go hand in hand with her.

She is cocky,
Bigoted,
Condescending,
Ruthless,
Hypocritical.

We call her Abilene, Texas.
I grew up with Abilene,
Walked across her bejeweled nerves
Dotted with shiny cathedrals,
Rode down
Her run-down highway veins
Watching her people consume
Themselves
In fake smiles.
Watching as
Pseudo-Christians drove their Cadillacs
Down her capillaries
Every Sunday morning
Thinking they will find
Enlightenment in churches

Specializing in guilt,
Giving to the needy only
To get to a higher place
In heaven.

As I grew
Her flashy ruby dress
Started looking less like pride
And a lot more like blood.

She was always an illusion
That only a child
With rose-colored lenses
Could ever see.

Somewhere between
Riding scooters down Peach Street
And moving boxes into Neeley dorms
Those glasses fell off,
Never to be worn again.

And then I saw her for the haggard,
Bitter old woman she really is.

So here I am, Abilene.

I'm no longer afraid to call you out on your bullshit.

Tell me, Abilene,
How you managed to hold
The world record
For most churches per capita
And the highest teen pregnancy rate
Across the nation
In the same year.

I know,
It's because of all the goddamned homosexuals and
Pot-smoking liberals that are ruining the nation
As you've told me before.

Of course it isn't the economic inequality,
Or social injustice,
Or corporations ,
Or hate in the name of religion
Shown by people like you
Who only know how to use Christianity

To condemn instead of to love.

Because it's much easier to hate
Someone you don't understand
Than trying to love a stranger unconditionally.

Tell me, Abilene,
Why you worship one socialist,
Long-haired hippie
But hate another,
Just because one is
The Son of God
And one is a
Son of the 70's.

Tell me how fucked up it is that
We have two hundred churches in this town
While there's also two hundred homeless on the street.

Tell me how you can be so opposed
To government intervention
Until it comes to gay marriage and abortion.

Tell me, Abilene,
What gives you the right
Telling people how to live
Based on your fundamentalist interpretations
Of a two thousand year old book
That no one can seem to agree on?
Instead of your annual bitching about
Putting the Christ back in Christmas,
Quit being a hypocrite and

Put the Christ back in Christian.

Tell me how it is
This country was founded
On exploring the unknown
Yet we're still afraid of what we don't know.

If you found a ghost haunting your hallways
But discovered it was a guardian angel
Would you still be afraid of it?

I say all this because
I know
You can do better, Abilene.

A lot of your people already have
Since we left.
Maybe we wouldn't
If you didn't keep giving
Us reasons to.

You don't have to keep hop-scotching
Over everyone
That doesn't fit
In your cookie-cutter box
And building up your cathedrals
Instead of building up your people.

You can turn yourself around, Abilene.

Instead be humble,
Tolerant,
Uplifting,
Merciful,
Genuine,
Trade in your stilettos
For some slingback sandals.
They make it a lot easier to breathe.

Take off that blazing red dress and
Slip into something simpler.
Something that doesn't remind your
People so much
Of fire and blood.

Something like . . . purple.

It's the perfect mix of red
And blue.

Madison Mae Parker

America the free, home of the brave
Has become
America the comfortable, home of the consumerist.
We build our cages out of trinkets and expensive goods
Because maybe if our mausoleum is nice enough
No one will question if we are living.

Suburbia:
How well does that 35 inch HD TV listen to you?
better yet:
How well do you listen to it?
better yet:
How well do you listen to your wife?
your kids?
your deaf ears are carving headstones
for your children's courage.
your work ethic
cannot replace
your love.

gluttons for comfort
gorging and purging
on ambulances carrying bombs
leaving your soul
searching for the noose
hidden in the alarm clock.

No, complacency is not the same as happiness.
No, numbness does not mean everything is all right.
Yes, I am terribly sad most days.
I have no idea why and no reason to be.
Yes, I eat too much and drink too much and read too little
and Love not enough.
I am guilty.

Suburbia.
You have made your slave.

You are a mirage
leaving your people holding
flasks filled with rusty feathers,
parched throats corked with half-truths
as the barrel of your eye dilates with closing of the curtain,
each slice of the credit card.

Citizens of the United Suburbans of America!
Your influence can stretch farther than your mailbox.
but fences become the vaults for your secrets,
tongues paint barbed wire across property lines.
God forbid
Picket lines
Threaten
Picket fences
because comfort has no need of change.

The American Dream.
She is a Siren.
by day
Her voice sounds of silken gold,
harps playing the emptiness to sleep.
by night,
A tsunami wave clenching apathy's lips.
She tastes like optimism drenched in whiskey.

you.
are drinking.
Her poison.
Her medicine has no need of child's locks.
for children know better than to be bogged down by their possessions.

Gibran once said,
*"Verily the lust for comfort murders the passions of the soul
and then walks grinning in the funeral."*

Your possessions will not attend your funeral.
They will not tell your stories in your absence.

Apathy is signing your own death certificate.

ignoring death
does not prolong
his coming.
it only taunts
His presence.

For Death is a drunken and disorderly mess.
He does not apologize.
He will not ask if you are okay.
he takes&he takes&he takes.

you will be left with
nothing.

empty your pockets now.
quit gripping everything
so tightly.

leave the enemy with nothing to shake loose from you
but
bones&blood
coffee&grease
oxygen&scars

Try everything
Fail something
Succeed at little
Live a lot
This is joy&sorrow mixed into one.

To live a happy life is to understand the weight of sadness.
Suburbia, do not fear your imperfections.

Hermann Rorschach

I look up and my mirror is a Rorschach test. The lines in my face spill of ink and black confetti. "Tell me what you see?" they say. "There are monsters hidden in the ink. Their screams are chartreuse dissonance bouncing inside my hollow bones." "Hallowed be thy name," they say. Their eyes *blinkblinkblink* back at me. Ink pours from their eyes and they scream, "Why don't you see a bat? A butterfly? Why don't you see the normal? The expected? The sane?"

I blink.

"C o u n t T o T e n ."
I see knives ripping open apples.
(It's really your esophagus.)
I see bombs exploding.
(We call them fireworks from so far away.)
I see oxygen tanks in your pens.
(When did breathing become such a challenge?)
I see bruises on the moon.
(I'm surprised we haven't blamed her for her wounds.)

"C o u n t T o Z e r o ."
Ink spills from my pen and I pass out from the loss of blood.
My stomach is filled with mortar.

I swallowed my home whole, too afraid to settle (down).
Loading a slingshot, my fears boomerang
back in resurrecting prophecies.
My depression is expressed in butterflies and sunrises
(even clichés need homes.)
I hold my breath 'til my life is played —
Rewind.
Slow down. Rewind. Slow down.
P a u s e :

if my life played in reverse
i would go to bed with the sun/ /kiss the moon good morning
every slur word would sound like *I'm sorry*
we would eat every word we speak/ /ears would tell the tales of others
showering would not be an act of cleanliness/ /a salvific moment, clinging
to the memories forever
flowers would grow into the ground/ /finally understand the meaning of
finding your roots
i would love my parents better because I would have been a parent first
my mother's body would not be a dry riverbed/ /a waterfall of wings
every last word/ /cry of first breath
art supplies would be created from art itself
musical notes creating strings and brass bands
understanding that

**Art
is Greater.**

than the two hands that manipulate
tones
words
colors
we would be birthed with hard knuckles, worn hands
allowing the world to soften us into the shape of
l o v e
the color black could finally disassociate himself with death for every
funeral procession would be a parade welcoming you
h o m e
there would be no question of heaven or hell
because we would have been where we always
b e l o n g e d

Justin Welsh

lugubrious

Blood Moon

I connect days together like constellations

mapping out numbers that will allow us to light the entire Earth.

And as my mind beats with the thrilling thought of you rolling over in

sheets of infinity,

I am certain the equation equals forever.

Now I connect our intimacy together like the bouquet of flowers on your

granite counter top

vaguely displayed and slowly decaying from their inability to care.

And as my heart releases to the thought of our rapid-fire-love that is shot

into infinity,

I am certain the equation equals never.

Garden Demons

When I peer into the garden
Exposed eyes are pardoned

The one I want is forsaken
Playing my cards so patient

Silently scuttling
As I swarm suddenly

Left alone after one by one
Enjoying the lilies and the chicken run
Approached from behind
With a petrified spine
I slide into thee a metal so dense
With forceful fingers right over his lips

We collapse to the ground with dagger in place
I swore to my love this vengeance would be faced

118

I peer upon a ghostly shell
With this thought I would prevail
This garden is evil and the gardeners who grow it
Because they work for a corpse whose evils have spoken

Austyn Degelman

Old Hymns

I used to run to the light as it faded until I saw you in the dark,
standin' there smiling like a Japanese moon,
piano strings pulled taut up your back to straighten out your spine.
I snuck over real slow, reached to pluck one while you weren't looking.
I wanted to scare you out of tune, loosen your bones,
but you saw me before I could. You saw everything.
How could you not?
Like you've got some kinda haunted chapels for eyes.

I was so afraid to get lost in them but I still took a look inside.
My footsteps echoed as I walked in
like they wanted to tell you I was coming,
saying, "Listen. She's finally here."
I looked to my right and saw us all stained-glass-light and red velvet
sittin' on the back row
singin' old hymns that we couldn't put names to.

Then you stopped to whisper in my ear,
"Am I your favorite song?"
Those words chimed in my head like holiday bells
and if I spin fast enough I can still hear them ringing.
I just asked you to sit up straighter;
spread my fingers across your ribs, played all the notes
thinkin' I could get used to this,
the way every bone in your body moves like polyphony.

Then I found a chord that spoke above everything else
and it sounded like, "Yeah . . . You are."
Then everything dissolved.

It turned into a cold sweat clinging to my skin

but it felt like frost,
and maybe the weather was bad, but listen.
Listen to the rain beat down
and tell me it doesn't sound like everything that we've lost
is running back home.

I opened the door to let it all in
and we celebrated their return with a dance.
Feet pressed, fluid and lockstep like they never even left.
Eventually we collapsed, exhaled into dust and sparks and all flickering
gold.
We slept arm in arm for an entire week until I woke up on a bed of sheet
music.

Love-letter-eighth-notes pressed into the sleep lines on my cheek like a
blueprint,
like they kissed me into a song and I became a home.
See, we can love so hard it'd make your neighbors
stop believing in
God.
They'd just sit in their kitchen on Sundays
with all the windows open
waiting on some kind of breaking that sounds like an old hymn,
whispering, "Please, carry on."
and the music sounds like the snapping neck of a violin,
a wild rumpus of feet dancing on cello strings,
like trombones splitting open to say you can still be reckless without a voice.
It's called giving yourself to someone and
it's terrifying.
To me, everything is terrifying.
That's why I'm having a hard time deciding
whether or not you actually exist.
Because you're the only thing I've never been scared of.
But your name still trembles when I hold it in my mouth
like a worry that if I speak

it'll only bleed into the wind and fade out.
I say it anyways and it tastes like a ghost passing
through my lips.

Every word I've said to you wraps around your shoulders
and I hope you get goose bumps.
I hope they shake you awake gently,
soak into you like a second skin.

Wear me like water wears moonlight,
ripple with each heartbeat and I'll refract.
I'm not breaking; I'm just bending to fit you.
See how I'm turning into a marimba?
Your fingers are the keys, all rosewood and stainless.
Every touch hums through the resonators
and I love it when you play wrong notes
'cause I get to show you the right ones,
like my collarbone, my shoulders, my neck.
Close your eyes,
lean against the storm door and remember all of my thunder.
Can you still hear me?

I know you'll leave soon but I'll be here when you get back,
sitting in the trees, dressed in my Sunday best
with a book of songs
waiting for the sun to fall down so I can say your name and
watch it run out of my mouth to chase the light as it fades.

Kiss me like a lantern festival,
siphon the beats from my heart and spit them
into your palm
like crystal teeth
all etched with the words
                    "break glass in case of emergency."

Throw 'em on the ground like fireworks;
listen to 'em pop and sizzle and sing.
They're talking about your eyes,
how they're soft like dirt and I want to be buried in them.
I'll even do the digging.

Wrap me up in your forest-fire-bones,
let the sinew of mine call yours a home.
I'll send smoke signals up your spine
asking your shoulders to give those piano strings some slack.
Relax, darling, settle down in this kick drum with me;
let it pedal us on home.
I'll murmur all those old hymns into your back,
the ones that we couldn't put names to.
My head won't stop ringing
with the words, "Am I your favorite song?"
So I press your ear to my heart
and I tell you to listen until it sustains the very last note.

The one that sounds like, "Yeah . . . You are."

How I'm Learning

I buried all of my sad and it turned into an orchard.
Leaking compassion, it turned into a forest,
dripping light, it turned into an ocean,
and I turned myself away from it.

I do not want to be anything other than the body I am now
even though it's not the one I want.
It is the only me that I have the strength to carry.

Wading through broken beer bottles on the floor
like a hundred shipwrecks,
I realize I can make anything look beautiful
if I just close my eyes and turn it into a metaphor.

So I made my depression a piano,
made my anxiety a bursting sun,
made it spill out of my hands and onto the keys
and . . . do you see where I'm going with this?
So you see how hard I try to make myself look like something
other than this body?

Because the truth is, I'm still learning
how to be a person
without wishing that I wasn't,
teaching myself that it's okay to always blush around strangers
and fall in love with them.

I am fragile and I am spinning
but no matter how much carousel I take out of me
I am always, always this body.
This body that is sometimes a whisper
and sometimes burning.

Sometimes a bruise, and sometimes a tongue.
Sometimes completely new skin,
but always missing the same things.
Sometimes transparent,
but never invisible enough to hide from the truth;

that as long as my eyes are open,
I will see myself as what I already am.
So I am learning to be beautiful without being a metaphor,
and that fragility is in the way you hold things
not in the way they break.

I'm gonna start breathing like things matter again.
I'm not going to change my name to an apology.

I'll bleed with purpose instead of hate,
turn back to face the ocean because it is also a body.
Even though the waves break
they are still made of the same thing
and I know I can do it too.

This isn't a poem; it's a promise.
I'll be the orchard and the forest and the sea,
and I will look beautiful to everyone who has their eyes open.

Garrett King

Big fish

I come from a town of fishermen. Not just because we were close to the gulf but because everyone left hooks in everyone else.

We were called forth to go out and be fishers of men. And that's what we do. There are some hooks that with a little fight get shook out easy and they get away. But there are others whose barbed personalities leave you stalking their Facebook and Twitter pages begging for the silver-lined-net that prove they're fighting just as hard as you. You can dive and try hiding under the boat but they'll always have that line right to you. And it's in there deep.

Home is full of both weathered captains and white whales. We search our oceans for each other, circling.

The sirens . . . their harpoon-bones support their tangled-net-skin, hair of flotsam and souls of jetsam. Rolling in the deep, they take to their coral churches and pray to end the emotional doldrums of their life.

You came from a long line of old men and seas. Both parts seasoned heart-angler and body-wrangler. You threw out your hook without any bait, and like a familiar hug I put that noose around my neck. These days I can't tell if I'm still diving or floating belly up. Either way, I'm waiting for you to reel me in and let me go.

Big boat

He was built like a boat. Unsinkable, they called him; he was titanic; royalty. And he sailed on. Rough waters could not drench the fires in his engine. His heart, a boiler fed by the dark, soot-covered-trophies from his younger days. His engine under the high pressure to perform turned coal into diamonds. The heat made his brow sweat. Black and brown smoke curls from his towers, never clear.

He rocks his sailors, just as his ocean mother taught him. She was deep, and he was surface. His father was wind, pushing him on when he ran out of fuel. He is between the sea and the sky. He will greet you with his bow but keeps his head turned up, navigating by starlight. His decks are adorned with musicians and sparklers. He was charming, a leviathan on pointed shoes surprisingly nimble for his stature.

She was his anchor . . . a fraction of his size but with a comparable strength. She was able to keep him in place though his engines still churned and pulled. She did not weigh him down, but merely let him feel the ocean move around him.

One day he will dive below water, sub marine. The sailors will rehire but his captain will stay. The lights will go out and he will breathe in the brine. He will get all choked up, dressed in a suit that finally fits. He was more than his ship, more than his name. But he was titanic; royalty.

Aleenah Spencer

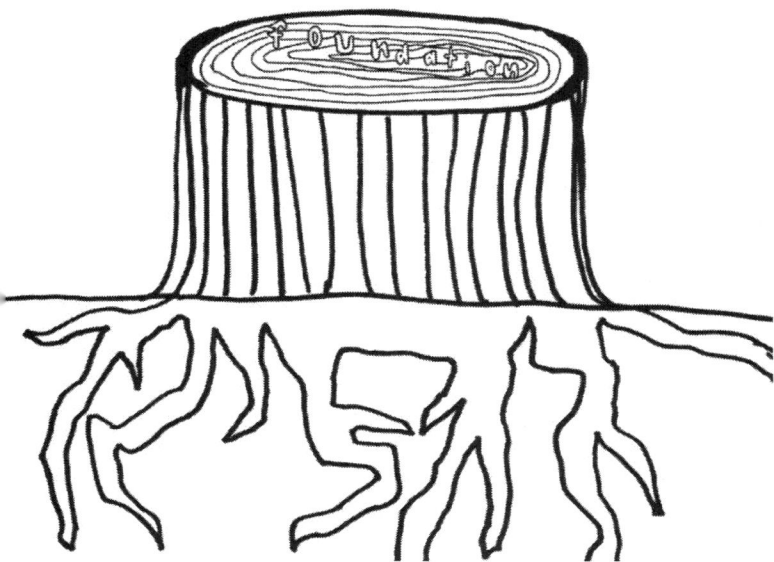

To Every Man Who Ever Thinks About Showing Interest in Me

Don't.

I am no damsel in distress.
I am, however, a damned soul.

Right off the bat I'll tell you . . . uh yeah, I have issues.
I don't like commitment.
It scares me.
This is me being open.
This is me being honest.

In response, you'll wrap your arm around me.
To you, it's comforting;
Really, you're strangling me.

When I get text messages in the morning that read:

> "GOOD MORNING BEAUTIFUL, smiley face explanation point
> less than three," I will be annoyed.

Don't ever do that shit again.

I am wishful thinking.
And suffocating.
And me.

TO EVERY MAN WHO EVER THINKS ABOUT EVER SHOWING
INTEREST IN ME

I'm warning you now.
It's not you . . . it's me.
Sometimes it's you . . .
Most of the time it's you.

When I tell you the first time I had sex, I was sixteen.
You'll judge me.

When I tell you it was rape.
You'll pity me.

I'm not sure which is worse . . .

Don't mistake your pity for guilt,

Questioning how you could have ever thought of me in that way.
I can see it.
In your eye's reflection, I can see me.
Sitting there.
I am guilt.
What'll really be a kick in the gut is when I tell you it happened a second time.
Fool me twice, shame on me, right?
. . you don't always learn from your mistakes.

21.
I am damaged goods.
And sloppy seconds.
And me.

TO EVERY MAN WHO EVER THINKS ABOUT EVER SHOWING INTEREST IN ME

My knuckles are scarred from holding my own.
I am complete.
And empty.
I don't have daddy issues.
I don't want your humble opinion.
Remove that heart from your sleeve,
Be frugal with your compliments,
That›s your dick talking.
Keep your ribs locked.
Keep your lungs full.
Keep your heels overhead.

And if I sleep with you
Count on me not being there in the morning.
But—

When I sleep with you, it will be a mistake.
You'll cradle me like the child I actually am and ask,
"Are you okay?"
"I'm fine. I'm okay."
I'll kiss you.
And roll over.
And cry.
I am vulnerability.
And broken.
And me.

TO EVERY MAN WHO EVER THINKS ABOUT EVER SHOWING
INTEREST IN ME,

I'll be frustrating.
          And a huge pain in the ass.
I am not a project.

Regardless, you will chip at my edges.
And weather me raw.
You will mess up.
          & it'll feel like sixteen.
I am hardened heart.
          & confusion.
                    & silence.

TO THE MAN WHO ONCE SHOWED INTEREST IN ME

I am sorry.

I will build this wall back up.
          & I will hand you a new chisel.

NEW SHIT

This poem smells a lot like secondhand guilt
From a firsthand smoker.
It is stray-dog-happy
Running through oncoming traffic.
It is just "to smile and pity it."
It is butchered imagery served raw: a lot to digest.
I will call it new shit.

This poem sounds like the language deafs think in: *hard to hear*.
It is puppy-mill-disgusting.
It is judging people more on their beliefs of the afterlife
And less on their basic human decency.

This poem is degrading your God to the form of man.
It feels like writer's block when writing a suicide letter,
Like someone calling it a blessing
When you worked your ass off on it.
I will call it speechless.

This poem feels like bare skin touched by bared arms.
Like racism continuously being excused for ignorance.
It is lower-middle-class voting-republican stupid.
This poem sounds like all the phones ringing in the rubble of the twin towers.
It is the NSA-before-9/11 useless.
It is the human race fighting one another with galaxies upon galaxies right there!
Let's take pride!
We will call it a civil war!

This poem is an existential crisis on acid.
Like wearing-white-pants-on-your-period-terrifying.
It looks like left arm amputee;
It is no sign of a war hero,
Just a product of shooting up too much heroin.

This poem is a requiem;
We will call it a dream.
This poem is a 6-year-old shoveling to China: like digging for knowledge.

It is spent lives fighting for rights
Just to fight one another.
It tastes bitter like the CIA and cocaine.

This poem sounds like,

   "There are more African Americans in prison today than were ever in slavery."

And it looks like activism in the form of Facebook.
We will call it profiling.

This poem is pre-occupation seeking occupation.
There will be no revolution.

This poem is monkeys with egos.
We will call it the human race.

We will call it —

Zach Lannes

Rejuvenation

Sitting at the ballpark
My old man said to me:

"   My old man said:

'Sometimes, I wonder why I do the things I do.
I wonder why I put up with an asshole boss
So obsessive over deadlines
Just to be worn to dreams,
Just to wear out
My slinky business shirts,
Ugly, putrid green.'

I think things get overcomplicated.
I wonder why I don't just take a trip
To a simpler place,
To help others   with the clothes I carry on my back,
And let them wear away
All the ugly, putrid green

Sometimes I wonder
Why I wake up in the mornings.
When I get in the pool
The first few laps are a struggle.
But as I swim I realize that I feel no troubles in the moment,
So liquid and clean.
And it is me and my thoughts
And my music
To get lost in.   "

(I think the ripples help him
Forget about the snags;
They disappear in
Destructive interference
Or like wrinkles when cloth is washed.)

'Sometimes I wonder
If god were to come down
Tomorrow and say,
"I'm taking you tomorrow,"
What would happen.
But I think I would be content
With how I had used what he had given me
To overcome the ugly, putrid green.

(The key in the execution, not the idea that I did)
And made it a beautiful collage of the days
And ways that experience defined me.'

When I asked how to handle losing life.

A Reflection

Say you were trapped in
The curly-headed loop of where you go next in
The grand scheme of that gal
You so loved the evening before
And morning after

Her irises, so solemn with
Pieces of the twinkly sky transported
Into that dark-pupil-gleam
That made you want to water your eyes
And spring up and proclaim:

"My lady is the sun, so bright in the sky
Who cannot be held by solely human view;
She is too bright for sheer human eyes
For she illuminates the earth with every subtle move.

She may disappear for a bit, I can say.
She is busy bringing life to others.
Well, I know that with me she always will stay
For she illuminates even her substitute shell.

I circle around her with great joy every day.
Others do as well, for 'tis the way of nature
To let us look in the most elevated way.
The beauties above our terrestrial stature
And your radiating beauty I truly cannot say,
But only try to poetically capture."

Or another verse form that sounds
Like it came from a few hundred years ago.
You want to take her to the place that you think she's worth
— You probably can't afford it in that case —
And show her the place she's worth saving for:
Inside your heart.
You probably can't show her in that case

(It would hurt to break open your ribs.)

You know that she's made from one of your bones,
Like the moon from the sun,
For you, by the nature of what you think.

But you know that she's worth
The shining symphony
Of "I love you's"
Or jazz band playing three choruses on
Some lady called Naima

The key lies in what you want to say.

"You make my day,
Make my eyes
Water, make my
Mind soar to the sky,
Soar to
The sun, soar
To the water,
Soar to the sky.
To the heavens,
Sore (you are)
The sun."

Brent Harrison

Miscellaneous Haiku

I swore to stop writ-
ing about you seventeen
syllables ago.

Tell yourself she does
not mean the world to you, now.
Lather, rinse, repeat.

My heart is an old
time villain, always leaving
me tied to train tracks

Your heart is a mass
grave where I will never find
a peaceful night's rest.

When grief rains, it pours.
If we don't drown, why do our
tears taste like the sea?

The loneliest nights
are the ones spent sleeping with
girls you'll never love.

I can pull all my
petals off, but your love will
always end with "not."

If our country's so
free, why do I still have to
wear pants in public?

What law says I can't
play children's music out of
a windowless van?

Creepiness is in-
versely proportional to
how much she likes you.

Pens cut deeper than knives,
but not enough to rip
your name from my heart.

I didn't sleep last night.
You don't deserve the dreams
you have made your home.

Girlfriend inflicted
dutch oven — an Indiana
Jones face melter.

You are a mold for-
ever growing in the cris-
per drawer of my mind.

Brad Hendrickson

LEGACY

FEROS FERIO

SOLA VIRTUS NOBILITAT

Fly on the Wall

I was gifted with mosaic sight
It is near 360° vision
A global perspective
It leaves this humble house flying,
Wondering what is the point of humanity
If you choose not to be humane?

How do you apes walk on two legs,
Balance on unmarked graves and apologies
Dragging one broken body in front of the other,
Soldiering down the same road again and again
In a downward spiral?
Even spinning tops eventually tumble

Unbalanced, you creatures will trip,
A forced bow to the divine you have long forgotten,
Balloon tied to a million caskets
Flailing all the way down
Still attempting to fly

You try to reach heaven

This requires wings

I see the truth,
Bulls in human skin

You may stand taller than snakes but you are still worms

False kings
You have no right to the throne,
Confusing power and privilege

Even lions know to keep their paws close to earth,
Avoiding the freedom God hung in the cursed tree

So why is it you fools swat at me?
Thou I may spend my days
Hovering over filth and stench?

I know to avoid the shit inside men's chests,
A hurricane of pain
That breaks down levies around your humanity
Still being a fly I am more grounded than you

I know
I know to keep my back flat, a table
With wings draped over a carapace like a cloth
So that I might be prepared to serve

Let knifes cut away at my abundance,
Strip from me 'til everyone is fat with content

Don't forget you're gifted with thumbs

They are meant to hold out charity

Not to wrap around your brother's throat
Or squeeze your sister's heart
Just because you can grasp something
Does not make it yours to hold

Left and right, they are weapons on a new family crest:
Skulls of your kin
Tears of your neighbors

They were meant to be tools
A hammer and nail
Building up everybody that crosses your path

You are also bare-skinned so that you cannot hide,
Naked and open to those around, and them to you
Leaving only breast and breath between beating hearts

Yet every day you build new walls
Fighting to be kings of a worthless hill

You could have worked together,
Climbed a mountain

But no
It is easier to dig a six foot hole than build a home

So I say buzz off,
Continue to strut like the blind drunk fools you are

May you stumble and fall 'til the day you don't get back up
Allow your hands and knees to touch the ground,
A reminder where you came from

Listen to this fly on the bathroom wall,
'Cause I see all your bullshit

James Church

HEALING

Handmade From Fools Gold

After speaking with an old friend about "relationships,"
She informed me I'll never be able to commit.
That my life is too circus tent for one person.
That I'm a matchstick with a mouthful of gasoline,
One flint short from a tree line frowning,
A mosh pit of flamethrowers,
A throat full of smoke signals,
Hear how speaking and burning
Sound the same
If we yell bright enough.

She told me I was never meant to be a boyfriend or husband;
I'm too good of a distraction for those with crooked hearts.
That my hands are ribbons to wrap around you,
My lips fools-gold;
My sheets are a crutch to assist you in walking away.
So go.

Because we twist our tongues into crowns
And adorn ourselves
With the words we wish others would tell us,
Like,
The truth.

But if honesty was our first language
Then we lost our voice in the first heart we stumbled out of.
We've all tossed back the words others uncork from their lips.
We're all a saloon floor,
One conversation away from falling into someone else,
Again
And again
And again.

We need to remember
None of us are diamonds.
We aren't enough coal mine to stand the pressure of loving Flawlessly,
Not enough ocean liner to know when to anchor down.
We are too human to understand our actions.
It's why we impersonate cardiologists for a chance to hold a heart.
This is where I'm guilty.
I haven't learned the difference
Between someone offering their heart and showing it.
I haven't learned how to speak in rhythm
With the chandeliers hanging in our chests.

Because my tongue is a tight rope with too much slack
My words are fraying.
It's why we unravel when told the truth.
That we're all slip knots loosing our grip.

I never needed someone to tell me how fucked-up I am,
But understand this:
I'm equal parts apology and confessional.
That after I burn
My heart won't stop beating.
It'll become fluent in smoke signal.
So after I age into a brass trumpet playing in tune of statue
Promise me this:

Bury my mistakes.

Etch on the tombstone:

"Here,

Here rests an adventure."

An Offering of Wine in D-Major

She makes me believe love
Is a curse
Man has given to themselves.
That caution shines on beauty the brightest.

The first time I kissed her
My heart stumbled by
Rattling its beggar's cup.
Her lips tasted like the grace from a lost gospel,
A miracle unknown to herself.
She loves wine;
I watch her uncork her lips and pour butterflies down my throat,
Their wings fluttering against my belly.
They sound like a wedding toast cocooned in my stomach.
Her hands are the ripped pages of a forgotten language;
My body transcribes her touch;
She's fluent in the expectations of another man's affection;
I'm learning to speak in rhythm with how her heart beats,
Learning her mind is a bear trap I choose to step on.

When I write,
She'll place her ear against my wrists.
A settlement of goose bumps will take refuge along my spine.
She hears every word rappel down my veins,
An army of inkwells loaded in my fingertips.
How do I tell her,
> "My chest is a collage of broken piano keys
> All trying to get back in tune?"
But when I see her
I can't help but play another song.
I hear
As Time Goes By creak beneath its ivory.
Of all the arms in all the towns in all the world
She walks into mine.

She,
She has her quirks.
Every time she leaves her room
She apologizes for not looking cute.

I tell her,
> "I'm a fool with a heart set on narcoleptic,
> A hibernating waltz waiting for its partner.
> Come keep rhythm with me."

Her frown crumbles like an empire.
She manages a smile.
It looks like the biggest truth she's ever told.
I reach for her hand
But I remember
Being the other man
Is a calf offering itself to the butcher.
That when we hold hands
Her wedding ring makes the first incision.
This is why my heart and brain
Refuse to speak to each other.
Because
How does one come to terms?

I don't.

Ignorance is a noose we hang the truth from.

So I pull up a chair,
Uncork another bottle of wine,
And wait.

Laura Welsh

Elephants and Owls

Somebody once asked me upon entering my house
Why all girls are obsessed with elephants and owls

I don't know

I just know

I keep an elephant figurine inside every room of my home

A gang member collecting time until his third strike told me his Overseer
tattooed a Lion onto his right shoulder looking down

He told me this is the reason I climb to high places in the night,

Because I like to look down, to be in control

I don't know

I just know

I don't often get too high anymore

But that doesn't stop me from wanting to feel closer to the sky

To look up at the vastness of space outside of my control

A friend asked me why

I'm always trying to prove something to myself

Said they were worried I would push myself so far

The fever of passion would burn out

I don't know

just know

Part of me is never more alive than when I'm hitting the ground

know that one of the first lessons they taught me

When I was sitting on a horse when I was three years old

Was the best way to protect my body when I'm falling down

just know that if I ever push myself so far

That the fever of passion burns out

will finally be satisfied enough to stay in one place

And stop sleeping with Ghosts

Boys and men have been telling me

There's something behind my eyes they long for,

Wish I would allow them to kno

don't know what they're talking about

It's not my fault that I can't break eye contact,

That I always stare for one second too long and too loud

A boy growing into a man, not yet in stable control

Looked my loud eyes in the mouth

And told me my mentality was more horse than human

Well, *I just know* horses' eagle eyes will never lie,

They always stare so loud

I learned to trust a species always on the verge of losing control

I *know* that body language is so loud

I *know* that on a sudden impulse

I tattooed the words "*ain't no grave*"

On the front side of my right hand

So that every time I write, or shake a strangers hand I remember

Ain't No Grave Ever Gonna Hold My Body Down

I *know* that I own thirteen clocks scattered around my house

And while their second hands tick throughout the night
Not a single one is set to the actual time
Or else I could not sleep within the walls of my home

A Marine suffering from PTSD told me that I was crazy

That these are the kind of insane, irrational compulsions that People come up with when they're trying to live with something, When they're learning to live with Ghosts

Well what I know is what I've been living through is life and

I have learned to speak the language

Of these ghosts outside of my control

I know that I did not get up on this stage so that we could feel Comfortable or in control

I quit taking Klonopin four years ago because I got nauseated by a Therapist telling me I would find the answers if I only looked down

But look up at me now

Fingernails and cuticles chewed to bloody shit,

I still can't quit smoking cigarettes

But I have not fallen to a panic attack yet

I know that I am most comfortably uncomfortable when my Awkward compulsions are uncontrolled

So

When you ask me why all girls are obsessed with elephants and Owls

Maybe

I'm just a little too obsessed wondering

If we will ever stand back up after we fall to death

I know that Elephants mourn the loss of their friends,
So I keep an Elephant in every room of my home
To remember my dead

Ryan McMasters

BRIDGES

Four Letter Words That People Are Numb to

Help — a request of assistance, a cry of urgency disregarded as "Your problem, not mine." Nobody responds to it if you're in immediate duress; somebody else is assumed to do so. The only attention you will get is if you scream,

"FIRE!!!" — a growing amount of energy that consumes everything it touches: dry tinder, a gas tank, your antique photo albums, your surprised loins. If something is burning it only makes *sense* to want to *drown* it *out*, to drench the covers that are being set ablaze by your fire even if you did not set the fire yourself,

"Stop!" — a command!
Not a compromise,
not a suggestion,
a ceasing of action. Sounds like, "Ask again later." , "You're not quitting that easily, are you?" , "Yellow means speed through the intersection of my legs before I turn red with

"Love" — a selfless action,
underrated.
A powerful force
gravitating with push & pull and so much compression it can suffocate, crush, or break. If you don't understand the power of passionate love and it's bestowed upon you against your will, when all you know is abuse it may be construed as unwanted, foreign, scary

Rape — the act of taking someone's choice and throwing it away with your chivalry, the discarded wrapper of the condom you didn't use, the entitlement which causes you to cower in flagrant assumption.

Riddle: When does "no" sound like "yes?"

Answer: When you want something bad enough.

When "body" sounds like "*receptacle*,"
like "*leftovers for dinner*," like "*ghost felony*,"
like "one night stand ends in one person standing & the other quivers & mumbles in fetal fear,"
when you see another person's form & think
"Mine." — A word connoting ownership, your immature thought process that it's your birthright to help with birth, *right*? Seeds sown like the streets are your concrete farm; "They won't grow on such solid soil, so who's it going to

Hurt?" — The word that encapsulates all the others, the easiest to feel, but one of the hardest to not feel *shame in*. It's understandable, but terrifying to not feel the blowback of another's insensitivity. It is far easier to feel nothing; the flaying of your vulnerability will hurt & is healthier but it is not often chosen when the other option is being

Numb.

Spoiler Alerts

When people get on stage and talk about their personal lives or feelings . . . we have this oooooone *little* problem. When we use honesty to sweat out the pain in the sauna of a stage, we become a walking advertisement of why you SHOULDN'T date us . . .

We don't need Truth Serum to be honest, we just need fewer crayons to make reality less pretty. We are the house sellers that are TOO EXCITED to talk about why such NICE houses SELL for so cheap.

"You see this here?!?! This is where the murder happened!! The blood **flew** like magician doves or cards being splayed on the blackjack table. It was just beautiful enough to **confuse** you. You know what they say, "The house always wins."

Unless you're creative.
Then
you see something for something it's **not**. You see a tragedy & you see a macabre masterpiece, you see a death as a punch line,
You see HAPPINESS &
. . .
You stare at it blankly.
It is not relevant to be happy.
We fixate on unhappy
because we can make ugly things pretty . . .
better than we can ever leave well enough alone.
We know how to be alone.
We're Lenny from Of Mice & Men:

we don't know our own strength.

We are strong, but we never know HOW strong
until we break something:

a Heart,   a Spine,

                        a Face,

                                                a Psyche,
a Body of work,   a Body,

            they all FRAGMENT under our fumbling exploration.

It's almost a sacrilege to think simply.
If there's not a Point to Make
or a Quip to Equip,
happy is of no use to us.
Just like Lenny, we will have to be held at gunpoint to look at the flowers.

Our love lives look like an EKG reading:

                        spikes,
            Flatline with occasional   back to flatline again.

We aren't looking for pristine people;
we're looking for broken mirror glass pieces
with the straightest edges
so when we cut deep enough to make a mark
but not enough to sever,
when we slice our skin to the prettiest of ribbons,
we can feel like we're dolling up the gifts that we are.

The biggest mystery of life to me is not whether there is a God, but how do people
not die alone?

 Full disclosure flaps in the wind like a white surrender flag.

We are the walking spoiler alerts.

By the time you meet me one on one,
I will wonder if I have anything intimate to give you
that hasn't been whispered into another person's ears

from a microphone stand.
By trying to solidify that other people should feel special,
I sometimes don't feel all that special.

Congratulations. You've witnessed a live self-fulfilling prophesy. Please
learn something from it
so at least somebody does.

Community Haiku

Doctors Are No Repairmen

My heart's an antique.
A 1992 model.
No natural spare parts.

–Brent C. Green

Response to Tova Charles'
Plain Gold Ring poem:

White man kills himself
Out of a tub; somebody
Else will clean it up.

Ryan McMasters –

Things I Bought at HEB at 4:30 AM

Cucumber
Chocolate Soy Milk
Tortillas
Double A's
Band-Aids

– Davis Land

Vyvanse

On morning tongue war
mint and coffee; teeth roll beats
named "necessity."

Christian Taylor –

Stereotypical Haiku

Poets wear all black
Poets drink strong black coffee
Poets are quite sad

Veronica Brady—

Pac-i-fist:

It means I
pass a fist
onto my other cheek
when it comes at me

— Brent C. Green

Honestly
I cannot think of any haiku
See what I did there

Amir Safi —

i won't follow you
into the sea because
i want to find it
myself

–Davis Land

This? All this dark? It's a suitcase
It's in your chest
Open it, honey

Good Ghost Bill–

One time, Regina George
Punched me in the face. I've liked
It rough ever since.

–Ryan McMasters

They say laughter is the best medicine . . .
Besides actual medicine.
Garrett King–

Tattoo marks him
Seventy years past expiration date.
Survivor.
— Sarah Maddux

see all that pretty out
there
don't you dare miss a bit,
don't you
dare
Davis Land —

I'm size 0 she
said. I asked what does that mean?
She said I'm nothing.
— Brent C. Green

Uncle says to Aunt,
"I am because you are. I
will be, 'cause you were."
Good Ghost Bill–

No Alcohol gods
require faith; they drink their
proof every time.
–Ryan McMasters

                                        Eden's forbidden frui
                                          Was not a red apple
                                            It was a cherry

                 Sarah Maddux –

He swims through all things,
It's what he was taught to do.
Even oceans end.
                    –Garrett King

                                  The ground the grass the
                                  gumbo the god the wate
                                    the weight you you you
                 Good Ghost Bill–

Dark stranger in alley.
Key clutched in my fist
Unlocks prejudice.
                    –Sarah Maddux

"You have a voice, and your voice is important."

This is the heart of Mic Check. We have tattooed this onto our voice boxes.

Mic Check is a 501(c)3 nonprofit organization that promotes and produces written and spoken-word poetry in Bryan, TX and the Brazos Valley area. More accurately, it is a graffiti hospital, a punk-rock church, an audience of ears and hearts and a stage all swung wide open for anyone with imagination and the gall to voice it out loud. Mic Check hosts weekly open mics, slams, and workshops; we speak in local schools about the power of writing, fundraise, organize community service, bring in poetry features from all over the nation, and host the annual Texas Grand Slam and Texas Youth Poetry Slam. We are safe haven and oasis for any wayward writer or audience member hungry for poetic substance and a creative outlet. We are your weekly reminder to tell your story, be loud, be proud, and most of all . . .

Speak or be spoken for.

40283555R00104

Made in the USA
Charleston, SC
02 April 2015